the simple guide to GROOMING
Your Dog

Eve Adamson
& Sandy Roth

T.F.H. Publications, Inc.

Distributed in the UNITED STATES to the Pet Trade by T.F.H. Publications, Inc., 1 TFH Plaza, Neptune City, NJ 07753; on the Internet at www.tfh.com; in CANADA by Rolf C. Hagen Inc., 3225 Sartelon St., Montreal, Quebec H4R 1E8; Pet Trade by H & L Pet Supplies Inc., 27 Kingston Crescent, Kitchener, Ontario N2B 2T6; in ENGLAND by T.F.H. Publications, PO Box 74, Havant PO9 5TT; in AUSTRALIA AND THE SOUTH PACIFIC by T.F.H. (Australia), Pty. Ltd., Box 149, Brookvale 2100 N.S.W., Australia; in NEW ZEALAND by Brooklands Aquarium Ltd., 5 McGiven Drive, New Plymouth, RD1 New Zealand; in SOUTH AFRICA by Rolf C. Hagen S.A. (PTY.) LTD., P.O. Box 201199, Durban North 4016, South Africa; in Japan by T.F.H. Publications. Published by T.F.H. Publications, Inc.

Contents

*Your Ally,
The Vet
Page 21*

Bathing Large Breeds Page 67

Treats and Toys for Better Teeth Page 85

Poodle Clips
Page 144–145

Shed and Mat
Page 178

Part One
The Importance of Good Grooming

"Just take a little off the top."

Good Grooming = Great Health

If grooming was all about beauty, we would probably still do it. Humans like to have clear skin, a sweet smell, thick shiny hair, and a really great haircut, and we like our dogs to look and smell great, too. But grooming is about more than good looks. Good grooming means great health, for both dogs and humans.

But while you know how to comb your own hair and take a shower, not all pet owners know or understand how to most effectively and efficiently groom their pets. Is your long-coated Shih Tzu a mess of tangles until you shave her down every spring? Is your Schnauzer a disheveled mess of stray wiry hairs? How is your Bearded Collie's

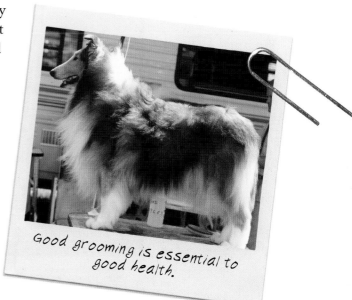

Good grooming is essential to good health.

skin under all that coat? And what about those wrinkles on your crinkly Pug? Are they dry and clean? Are your Beagle's ears free from infection? Have you figured out how to resolve that annoying hotspot on your yellow Lab? (If *you* think it's annoying, just imagine how your Lab feels!)

Grooming is directly related to health in many ways. A matted coat can hide and aggravate a host of skin conditions, which may in turn signify more serious health problems. A dull or balding coat can reveal medical conditions, such as hypothyroidism (symmetric hair loss is a clue), mange (a parasitic condition), or nutritional deficiencies (low protein could mean dull, sparse hair). Dogs with skin folds, floppy ears, furry paw pads, protruding eyes, flat faces, or dental issues all need special kinds of care as well.

Living with a dog is about much more than a daily walk, fresh food, and clean water. To keep your friend at his healthy best, thorough and targeted grooming is in order, and this book is here to help you understand exactly what your pet's individual grooming needs are, as well as how you can best meet them.

Head · Eyes · Stop · Ear · Nose · Mouth · Neck · Chest · Elbow · Forelegs · Back · Ribs · Tail · Stifle · Hock · Paws

Anatomy vis-à-vis Grooming

To best groom your dog, it helps to understand a little bit about dog anatomy first. Although a Pug looks a lot different than a Greyhound and a Chihuahua doesn't much resemble a Mastiff, all dogs share the same basic anatomy and many of the same anatomy-related grooming needs. Using the diagram for reference, let's consider the dog's anatomy as it relates to grooming.

The Head

A dog's head is an important area for grooming. Some dogs have protruding eyes, some have flat faces, and some have skin wrinkles, and each of these special features requires special grooming. A dog's eyes should be kept clean, eyes and nose checked for discharge, and his teeth cleaned and checked for excess tartar and gum infection. Dogs with floppy ears are prone to infection because bacteria and moisture can become trapped in the ear, but even prick-eared dogs can get infected or parasite-plagued ears. Dogs whose ears drag along the ground while they are hot on the trail of a scent (like Bloodhounds, Basset Hounds, and Beagles) may also get burrs and dirt in and on their ears.

Be careful to keep your dog's skin clean and dry.

Different dogs have different head shapes. Brachycephalic dogs have flat faces (think Pugs, Pekingese, Bulldogs, and Boston Terriers) and are more likely to have large, sometimes protruding eyes and facial wrinkles. Dogs with longer faces and more deeply set eyes (think Basenjis or Vizslas) may have fewer facial grooming needs, but still require vigilance to check for discharge from eyes and nose as well as healthy teeth and gums.

Stop Right There!

Some dogs have a distinct angle between skull and muzzle, called a *stop* (think the apple-domed Chihuahua), while some dogs have so little stop that the skull seems to flow directly into the muzzle. (Remember Spuds McKenzie, the Bull Terrier?) Other dogs fall somewhere along the middle of the spectrum, such as Labrador Retrievers with their moderate stop and Greyhounds with their gently subtle stop.

To keep your dog's face, (no matter what its shape) healthy and well groomed, wipe your dog's face clean with a damp cloth and make sure any folds and wrinkles stay clean and dry, as they can harbor bacteria and can become easily irritated. The flews (the pendulous skin at the corners of the mouth) on the lower lip, especially, need to be cleaned. Whiskers on a dog's muzzle can be trimmed, ear hair can be plucked, and muzzle can be otherwise neatened, but these are optional, although aesthetically rewarding, grooming chores.

The Body

Your dog's body may be low to the ground or towering, long or short, and covered in just about any kind of coat, from short to long, straight to curly. Though the head and paws may require more targeted grooming time, your dog's body is the realm of the skin and coat and must be tended for a healthy, shiny, vibrant appearance. Brush along the back, the neck, the chest, down each leg, and along the tail, if your dog has a tail. The belly of the male should be kept short for sanitary purposes.

Brushing or combing your dog is an aesthetically pleasing chore and a chance for you to appreciate your breed's unique shape, topline, tail set, and waist. (What, no waist? An overweight dog is prone to many additional health problems, so make good nutrition a partner to good grooming.)

A dog's coat grows in cycles and sheds at the same times every year.

Your dog's coat–his most striking feature–grows in cycles. Each hair follicle has a rapid growth phase, a slower growth phase, a resting phase, and a shedding phase. These phases differ in length according to breed, but most dogs shed or "blow" their coats once or twice a year, and in females, about six to eight weeks after giving birth.

Exposure to daylight can influence the coat growth cycle, so that dogs spending a lot of time outdoors are more likely to shed in regular cycles, whereas indoor dogs exposed to about the same light, thermal heat, or air conditioning all year-round may shed in less obvious cycles and be more likely to shed small amounts all year long.

Some dogs have a double coat, or a soft, wooly undercoat under a harder, shinier outer coat. These double coats offer double protection against the elements for working dogs, but the undercoat can shed in great tufts when the dog sheds.

Some curly-coated breeds don't shed in the same way other dogs shed. Long-coated dogs that shed develop mats more easily because when the long hairs or undercoats shed, they get caught in the longer hair and never drop off, causing tangles. Regular brushing and combing can dramatically reduce the annoyance of shed hair in the house by purposefully removing shed hair before it falls, not to mention minimizing the occurrence of mats.

For more on how to brush and comb your dog's coat, check later in the book for your dog's particular type of coat.

In the End

One part of your dog's body that you may not be so inclined to examine too thoroughly is the rear end. Dogs with long hair can develop mats in the rectal area, trapping fecal matter, and this area should be kept clipped and clean. All dogs also have anal glands that should empty on their own during defecation, but if your dog becomes irritated in this area or starts scooting around on the floor, these sacs may need to be emptied by hand (a common problem in many dogs). It's not a pretty job, but it isn't difficult, either. Ask your vet to demonstrate how to squeeze the fluid from these sacs. (If you take your dog to be professionally groomed, don't expect your groomer to do this job, and if she does, well...give her a nice tip!)

The Feet

Your dog has four paws, and each of those paws must be kept in good condition. Some dogs have tight, compact, rounded *cat feet* with a shorter third toe. These neat feet are easy to lift and make for greater endurance, as they are efficient for working dogs. Some breeds with cat feet include Doberman Pinschers, Newfoundlands, Finish Spitz, and Bichons Frise.

Some dogs have *hare feet,* which are more elongated, with two center toes longer than the side toes. Hare feet make for fast action and are characteristic of the speedy sighthounds like Greyhounds and Whippets. Other hare-footed breeds include the Samoyed, the Bedlington Terrier, and the Papillon. Many breeds have feet moderately between the cat foot and the hare foot. Some dogs stand well up on their toes, and others do not.

Some water dogs, such as the Chesapeake Bay Retriever, the Portuguese Water Dog, and the German Wirehaired Pointer, have webbed feet to help move them efficiently through the water to retrieve game.

The hair between the foot pads should be trimmed regularly to prevent matting.

Heel!

All dogs walk on their toes in the manner of a horse, instead of on the "soles" of their "feet" like humans. This means the dog's true "heel" is up in the air, not on the ground. The dog's paw is equivalent to the toes and ball of the human foot.

Some long-haired breeds grow hair between their foot pads, which should usually be trimmed away to prevent matting and ice caking in the winter, except in the case of some sled dogs, for whom this paw-pad hair serves a protective purpose.

Many dogs are born with dewclaws–fifth toes a few inches up the leg from the four toes on the floor. This vestigial toe serves no purpose and in many breeds–especially working breeds–the rear dewclaws are removed to prevent them from tearing off by accident. In other breeds, dewclaw removal is purely cosmetic. Many breeders have dewclaws removed, except for those breeds that are required to have them, according to their breed standards. All claws, including dewclaws, should be trimmed.

Grooming for Overall Health

We all want our dogs to be healthy, and while genetics, diet, exercise, attention, and mental stimulation all play a part in the big health picture, grooming is one important way you can directly affect your dog's health. A well-groomed dog is likely to maintain a healthier coat, skin, eyes, ears, teeth, and even structure.

Throughout this book we will go into lots of detail about how to groom your dog from nose to tail, no matter his size, shape, age, breed, and coat type, but let's look first at how basic grooming can affect the health of your dog in specific ways.

Coat Care

The coat is one of the dog's most variable features from one breed to the next. Shave them down and a Standard Poodle, an Afghan Hound, and a German Shorthaired Pointer don't look all that different, but put that Standard Poodle, Afghan, and German Shorthaired Pointer in their full show coats, and you'll see how different similarly sized dogs can look.

One of the most obvious indicators of good health in a dog is its coat. Whether your dog has a long, flowing coat; a mass of frizzy curls; or a sleek, shiny, hard coat, the condition of a dog's coat is the first thing most people notice, and it may be the first thing to deteriorate when a dog suffers from a health problem.

A poor coat could signify a systemic disease, or it could stem from poor grooming habits, instigating other problems. Caring for your dog's coat does more than keep it in good condition. It keeps you in contact with your dog, so that you can catch changes in his coat and skin more quickly. Coats must be washed, although some breeds require more frequent washing than others. Coats must be brushed, and long coats must be periodically detangled. Condition dry coats to keep hair pliable and to keep breakage to a minimum, and when it comes to good health, if you aren't willing to care for a long coat, keep it cut or shaved down. Your pet's comfort and good health are more important than sporting a long coat that isn't well groomed.

A well-tended coat free of mats and tangles and kept clean and parasite-free helps reveal skin problems when they begin, rather than hiding them until they are advanced, and will in itself prevent many skin problems from occurring in the first place.

An ungroomed coat can be the catalyst for many different health problems. Let's look at what can happen when you don't properly groom your dog.

The coat is often your dog's most recognizable feature.

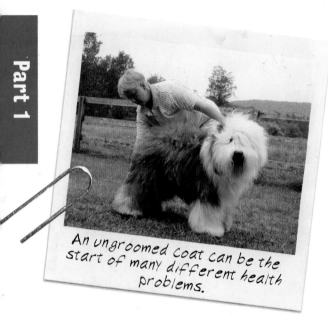

An ungroomed coat can be the start of many different health problems.

• **Mats:** Those knotty tangles in long coats caused by shed hair that wasn't shed all the way out are the result of a lack of adequate grooming, or of grooming done improperly. They are more than uncomfortable and unattractive. Mats can hide skin problems, from fleas and hot spots to tumors and abscesses.

• **Fleas:** Fleas can thrive underneath an ungroomed coat, and if you never wash or comb them out, they can breed quickly and infest your entire house. Flea bites can cause dermatitis on your pet, including itchy spots that can become badly infected. Fleas also carry diseases like bubonic plague, and their own parasites, such as tapeworms, that can infect your dog.

• **Ticks:** These blood-sucking arachnids look like harmless little beetles until they attach to your dog and swell with blood. Ticks contain harmful bacteria that can even infect humans if they burst during removal. They can also spread diseases to both dogs and humans, such as Lyme disease and Rocky Mountain Spotted Fever. If ticks are removed improperly, they can leave their heads inside your dog, and these wounds can become infected.

• **Poor hair quality:** Handling your dog's coat too roughly, bathing too often without conditioning, or using tools in the wrong way can result in breakage and brittle hair. Part of good grooming is good nutrition, and an unbalanced diet can also result in dry, brittle hair that breaks easily and looks dull and lifeless.

If you keep your dog's coat well groomed, it should be shiny, fluffy, smooth, clean, and pest-free. You should be able to run a flea comb through it without getting stuck, and it should be pliable and strong enough to resist breakage from regular brushing or combing. This is easy to accomplish by keeping your dog's skin and coat clean. In addition, check periodically for parasites, and run your hands over your dog's entire body at least once a week to check for any lumps, bumps, dry patches, sores, or other skin changes. You may also be able to determine other body issues such as pain in the hips, which could signify hip dysplasia; pain in the spine, which could signify disc disease; or other joint issues such as arthritis or slipping kneecaps. Just by touching and paying attention to any indications that your dog is in pain, you could catch a serious problem before it becomes much worse.

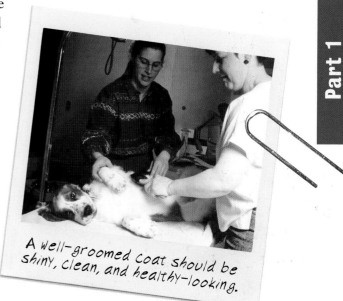

A well-groomed coat should be shiny, clean, and healthy-looking.

A beautiful coat, no matter what the length or texture, makes a dog look better, brighter, and healthier, and that's what good grooming is all about.

Skin Care

Underneath all that coat is your dog's largest organ: her skin. Coat care and skin care go hand in hand, and when one is healthy, the other is likely to be healthy, too. However, some breeds are more likely than others to suffer from skin problems, including allergies and reactions to irritants like flea bites, shampoos, and other environmental agents.

Some dogs have very dry skin or allergy-prone skin, and some breeds (such as certain scenthound

Coats of Many Colors

Dogs come in a huge range of colors, from white to black, blue to gold, lemon to red, and in many different patterns, from bi-colored to tri-colored to brindled, spotted, ticked, and roaned. Some grooming supplies are specifically designed to bring out your dog's best color: brightening shampoos for white coats, shampoos designed to bring out the gleam in black coats, and those made just for the lightest straw, the purest blue, or the deepest bronze.

Skin Cancer Check

Just as you keep an eye on your own hide to check for strange or changing lumps, bumps, and suspicious moles, you should also keep an eye on your dog's skin for signs of skin cancer. According to one estimate, 450 out of every 100,000 dogs is diagnosed with skin cancer, and light-coated dogs are more susceptible than those with dark coats, in the same way light-skinned people are more susceptible to skin cancer than dark-skinned people. Skin cancer is the most common type of cancer in dogs, so keep an eye out and talk to your vet about any suspicious moles, lesions, lumps, or other skin changes on your dog.

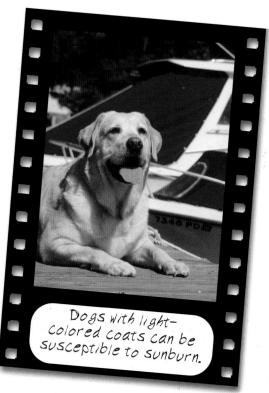

Dogs with light-colored coats can be susceptible to sunburn.

breeds) secrete oils that give them a strong odor if they aren't bathed frequently. Some dogs are prone to benign cysts, especially when they age; cysts and sores can also indicate certain serious medical conditions.

Dogs with white coats are prone to sunburn and should be sprayed with sunscreen made just for dogs. Dogs with black coats can easily become overheated, and moles and other skin abnormalities, including fleas and ticks, may be less obvious on a dark-coated dog. Any dog can develop skin cancer, especially those who spend a lot of time outside, so part of grooming should include a once-over to check your dog's skin for changes.

Eyes, Ears, Noses, and Teeth

You love your dog's beautiful face, and good grooming will keep that face beautiful and healthy. Eyes can tear, and many white dogs such as Maltese and white Poodles may develop tear stains. Other breeds, such as the Shih Tzu, tend to have dry eyes and may need a daily dose of moisturizing eyedrops to keep their eyes comfortable and healthy. Dogs with large, protruding eyes also require caution during grooming, as their eyes are relatively unprotected and could be injured with a misjudged manipulation of a grooming tool.

Dogs with long, floppy ears need special ear care to prevent infection, but all dogs can use an occasional ear cleaning. For dogs whose ears tend to grow hair, ear plucking will neaten the appearance of the head and could also prevent dirt and foreign matter from becoming trapped in the ear.

Check your dog's nose for discharge, which could indicate a respiratory problem or allergic reaction, and keep your dog's teeth clean; dental bacteria can travel to the heart where it can be deadly. Chew toys, like Nylabones®, can help keep his mouth healthy.

More on how to care for your dog's eyes, ears, nose, and teeth is discussed later in the book.

Paws and Claws

When claws get too long, they can compromise movement by bending the foot back too much and splaying out the toes. Too much walking on too-long toenails can eventually cripple a dog. Sharp claws can also do damage to human skin.

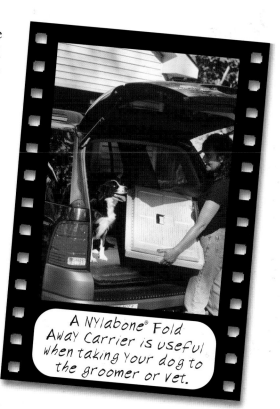

A Nylabone® Fold Away Carrier is useful when taking your dog to the groomer or vet.

Paw pads can become cracked and dry in dry weather or after walks on snow and ice. De-icing salt can also irritate or even damage a dog's paw pads, so keep paws neat, clean, and dry. Clip nails parallel to the ground, avoiding the vein, known as the quick, that extends part way down each nail.

A more detailed description of how to clip your dog's nails is discussed later in the book.

Your Ally, the Vet

Finally, no discussion of grooming for health would be complete without a note about your friendly neighborhood veterinarian. Regular vet care is essential to any pet's good health, but a vet can do more than vaccinations and a once-over. If you have questions about hygiene, concerns about odor or lumps or hair loss or tooth decay, or any other questions regarding your pet's skin, coat, nails, ears, or any other aspect of your pet's anatomy, even if it seems purely cosmetic, don't hesitate to ask your vet. Your vet may also be able to recommend a competent and experienced groomer to help you keep your pet looking his bright and shiny best.

Different Coats for Different Folks

What dog coat strikes your fancy? Do you adore the long flowing silk of a Yorkie or swoon over the powder puff head of a Bichon Frise? Maybe you admire the elegance of the Doberman's shiny, hard coat or are patently charmed by the whiskery, wiry look of a Schnauzer.

If you are reading this book, you probably already have a dog. Did you consider coat type when researching breeds? Coat type is an important consideration in choosing your pet because different coat types require drastically different grooming techniques–techniques you may or may not be willing to perform (or pay someone else to perform). You can brush down your

Coat type is an important consideration when choosing a breed.

Whippet with barely any effort, but to groom a Poodle on your own is a massive undertaking most pet owners prefer to delegate to a professional groomer (although learning to do it yourself can also be a lot of fun!). Of course, even if you chose a dog whose coat is more work than you thought it would be, you can always streamline your grooming chores. Find out how later on in this book.

In this chapter, we will look at the five basic coat types and talk about the nature of each coat, and what that means for the home groomer: You! Later on we will devote a chapter to the nuts and bolts of grooming each coat type, but here we'll get ready by looking at the coats themselves, the breeds that sport them, and how much care they involve.

The Smooth Coat

Smooth coats are shiny, sleek, and almost give the appearance of gleaming skin. They fit so closely that they don't interfere in any way with the sleek silhouettes of the breeds that sport them. Smooth coats are easy to groom: just brush, polish, and go.

Smooth coats should be short, sleek, and shiny.

Every group of purebred dogs, from sporting dogs to working dogs, terriers to toys, include breeds with smooth coats. Although they don't offer much protection from the elements compared to some other coat types, smooth coats also don't interfere with work, don't attract burrs, don't catch in the underbrush, and don't tangle or mat. Dogs with smooth coats are easier to care for in many ways. Wounds and parasites are easily visible and easily removable on a smooth coat, and smooth hard coats shed dried mud and debris with little more than a good shake.

Because smooth coats don't offer much skin protection, some smooth-coated breeds may develop irritated skin and some are prone to skin allergies. Unless they get into something really nasty, smooth-coated breeds don't normally require bathing more than a couple of times each year (with the exception of those dogs often out in the field working and getting dirty). Too much bathing can strip the oils from the skin of smooth-coated dogs, leaving skin more vulnerable and coat dull.

Some smooth-coated breeds have single coats and some have double coats, but undercoats shouldn't show through the hard outer coat. To keep smooth coats glossy, brush with a regular, natural bristle brush or a hound glove. A rubber curry brush can also help to loosen excess coat during shedding. Unlike heavier double coated breeds and breeds with longer coats, smooth coats don't require blowdrying, although a professional groomer may dry the smooth coats with a cage dryer to speed up drying. Smooth coats generally dry quickly, however.

Smooth-coated breeds are perfect for people who don't want to spend much time grooming, and who appreciate the clearly defined shape of the dog unencumbered by hair. Except for the occasional whisker trim, smooth-coated breeds are shown in dog shows "naturally," meaning their coats aren't groomed or shaped in any way.

Smooth-Coated Breeds

American Foxhound	Chinese Crested	Labrador Retriever
American Staffordshire Terrier	Dalmatian	Manchester Terrier (Toy and Standard)
Anatolian Shepherd	Dachshund (smooth)	
Basenji	Doberman Pinscher	Mastiff
Basset Hound	English Foxhound	Miniature Pinscher
Beagle	Fox Terrier (smooth)	Pointer
Black and Tan Coonhound	French Bulldog	Pharaoh Hound
Bloodhound	German Shorthaired Pointer	Pug
Boston Terrier	Great Dane	Rhodesian Ridgeback
Boxer	Greater Swiss Mountain Dog	Rottweiler
Bulldog	Greyhound	Staffordshire Bull Terrier
Bullmastiff	Harrier	Toy Fox Terrier
Bull Terrier	Ibizan Hound	Vizsla
Chihuahua (smooth)	Italian Greyhound	Weimeraner
Chinese Sharpei	Parson (Jack) Russell Terrier (smooth)	Whippet

Medium-Coated Breeds

Akita	Cardigan Welsh Corgi	Norwegian Elkhound
Alaskan Malamute	Cavalier King Charles Spaniel	Pembroke Welsh Corgi
American Eskimo Dog	Chesapeake Bay Retriever	Saint Bernard
Australian Cattle Dog	Clumber Spaniel	Saluki
Australian Shepherd	Collie (smooth)	Schipperke
Belgian Malinois	English Springer Spaniel	Siberian Husky
Belgian Sheepdog	Field Spaniel	Shiba Inu
Belgian Tervuren	Finnish Spitz	Spinone Italiano
Bernese Mountain Dog	Flat-Coated Retriever	Sussex Spaniel
Borzoi	German Shepherd Dog	Tibetan Spaniel
Border Collie	Golden Retriever	Welsh Springer Spaniel
Brittany	Great Pyrenees	
Canaan Dog	Kuvasz	

The Medium Coat

Medium-coated breeds are also easy to groom. They have coats generally longer than one inch but are by no means long. Medium-coated dogs don't generally develop mats, although thick double coats of this length could develop mats if they aren't brushed out once a week. In medium-coated dogs, the coat does stand out as part of the silhouette, but these breeds are also generally shown in natural form in the show ring, rather than requiring lots of trimming and other coat alteration.

Medium coats vary, from the silky feathers of a Golden Retriever to the plush fur of a Dandie Dinmont Terrier, the well-insulated Alaskan Malamute to the weather-resistant German Shepherd Dog. While medium-coated breeds may differ greatly from one breed to another, they all have one thing in common: a thick, weather-resistant coat evolved for survival in the elements (ice and snow, underbrush, or lake water). Many working and herding dogs have medium coats because these coats are easy to care for and don't interfere with the work at hand (or paw), but are thick enough to offer protection against cold and rain. Double-coated, medium-length coats are extra warm and water-repellent.

Brush medium coats thoroughly once a week and when parasites are a problem, apply a flea comb. Otherwise, these coats virtually take care of themselves—and the dogs that wear them. Medium-coated breeds are perfect for people who don't want to do much grooming and those who like larger dogs—many of the larger working, sporting, and herding breeds have medium coats. Medium-coated dogs are soft to the touch and easy to pet, perfectly embodying many peoples' idea of the perfect dog.

The Long Coat

The long coat is the grooming aficionado's dream coat. Witness any devoted groomer brushing out a Yorkie, an Afghan, or a Pekingese, and you'll know what we mean—and if you have a long-coated dog, you already know what we mean! Grooming a long coat is time-consuming but rewarding because the end result—a glamorous, flowing mane—is nothing short of breathtaking.

Medium-coated dogs vary in their grooming requirements, but all need brushing to look their best.

Some long coats are parted down the back and some aren't. Some are long and frizzy like a Chow Chow or a Pomeranian, or fluffy all over like a Collie or a Saint Bernard. Some have shorter coats along the back but long feathers along the underside, ears, and tail, like an English Setter. Long coats are a lot like human hair, and brushing and combing them can be quite similar to brushing and combing your own hair.

Why do dogs have long coats? Theories abound, but some believe that herding dogs tended to have long white coats in order to better blend in with flocks of sheep, and sheep-like coats offered protection from the elements. Some toy dogs probably evolved to have long, luxurious coats for the sake of the amusement of the royalty that kept and bred them, and to make them look regal and pampered. Over the centuries, as different breeds

Long coats need extra attention and a daily grooming routine.

evolved, long-coated breeds were probably selected for their beauty, as humans have long appreciated the aesthetic pleasures of a long-coated dog, whether on the hunt or riding around in the sleeve of a kimono.

Long coats do need fastidious attention every day, or at least every couple of days. Brush them, then comb with a flea comb to make sure all tangles are removed. Tangles left untended can trap shed hairs and can quickly turn to mats, and a long-coated dog with a matted coat is a sorry sight. Long coats also need bathing much more frequently than smooth coats, which require the skin's natural oils to maintain shiny health. Long-coated dogs are at greater risk for tangles, and a monthly bath, conditioning, and blow-out will keep this challenging coat type in great shape.

Long-Coated Breeds

Afghan Hound	Gordon Setter	Polish Lowland Sheepdog
Bearded Collie	Havanese	Pomeranian
Briard	Irish Setter	Saint Bernard (longhaired)
Chihuahua (longhaired)	Japanese Chin	Samoyed
Chinese Crested (powderpuff)	Keeshond	Shetland Sheepdog
Cocker Spaniel	Lhasa Apso	Shih Tzu
Chow Chow	Löwchen	Silky Terrier
Collie (rough)	Maltese	Skye Terrier
Dachshund (longhaired)	Newfoundland	Tibetan Terrier
English Cocker Spaniel	Old English Sheepdog	Yorkshire Terrier
English Setter	Papillion	
English Toy Spaniel	Pekingese	

Some long-coated dogs have long *long* coats, and some have coats that need lots of care but aren't quite as taxing to groom. Your Bearded Collie or Afghan will take a lot more combing than your long-haired Chihuahua or Papillion.

Long-coated dogs are perfect for people who love to spend lots of time doting on their pet via long grooming sessions. These sessions can be great ways for people and pets to bond. However, if you aren't up for the big grooming commitment but your heart is set on that Shih Tzu, Lhasa Apso, or Maltese, consider keeping your pet in a puppy cut or other short pet trim. For a show dog, only the most glorious of long coats will do, but for a beloved pet, coat length won't affect how much your dog loves you.

The Wirehaired/Broken Coat

The wirehaired or broken coat has a texture all its own: hard, coarse, and wiry. Wire-haired breeds are often groomed to sport jaunty beards, and their coats have a characteristic tousled look that some of us find irresistible.

Many breeds of terrier have a wire coat, and so do a few sporting dogs and hounds. Wire coats are incredibly weather-resistant. They defy burrs to stick in them and offer good protection for those dogs whose function often involved plummeting through harsh bracken, into burrows, or through fields in harsh climates after vermin, whether rats, badgers, or deer.

Many terrier breeds have broken or wire-haired coats.

The unique feature of a wire coat is that in order to keep it properly harsh and crisp, it should never be shaved down. Instead, it should be stripped or plucked, a process in which dead hairs are pulled by hand or with a stripping knife from the coat. Shaving down a wire coat can result in a softer, less characteristic texture, so wire-haired show dogs are almost always lovingly hand stripped by their owners, handlers, and/or groomers.

Wirehaired/Broken-Coated Breeds

Affenpinscher	German Wirehaired Pointer	Otterhound
Airedale Terrier	Schnauzer: Giant, Standard, and Miniature	Petit Basset Griffon Vendeen
Australian Terrier		Scottish Deerhound
Border Terrier	Irish Terrier	Scottish Terrier
Bouvier des Flandres	Irish Wolfhound	Sealyham Terrier
Brussels Griffon	Parson (Jack) Russell Terrier (wirehaired)	Soft Coated Wheaten Terrier
Cairn Terrier		Welsh Terrier
Dachshund (wirehaired)	Lakeland Terrier	West Highland White Terrier
Dandie Dinmont Terrier	Norfolk Terrier	Wirehaired Pointing Griffon
Fox Terrier (wire)	Norwich Terrier	

People who love the look of a wire-haired dog may enjoy the satisfying task of hand stripping, either a lot at a time several times a year, or a little bit at a time all year long. However, if you love your wire-haired friend but don't want to engage in the time-consuming effort of hand stripping your pet, periodic clipping and the resultant softer coat may be a perfectly acceptable option.

The Curly or Wavy Coat

So few breeds with curly coats, *so much grooming!* Although curls characterize just a handful of breeds, they present a unique grooming challenge. Most pet owners take their curly-coated pets to a professional groomer, because the grooming of a curly coat is difficult and takes practice. Luckily, the curly coat grows back in quickly, making it the perfect canvas for the novice groomer. You can practice…and practice…and practice until you achieve perfection.

Groomers spend much of their time learning how to groom a single breed: Poodles! Whole books have been written about Poodle grooming (you won't find a whole book devoted to grooming the Labrador Retriever!). Grooming a curly coat takes skill with a clipper and scissors to achieve the clip of choice.

Some curly-coated breeds sport dreadlocks. The large white Komondor and the diminutive Puli are two distinctively corded breeds with curly coats that fall naturally into cords who would look a lot like Poodles if they were groomed that way. Similarly, a Poodle could wear a corded coat if its curls were allowed to form into cords, and, in fact, the corded Poodle was in fashion in the 19th century.

How a curly coat will be groomed is largely a matter of fashion and practicality for an individual breed. The Poodle's characteristic balls of fur around its joints originally served the function of protecting joints from cold water, as Poodles were once water retrievers. The Poodle wasn't left in full coat because the sheer weight of the coat would have made swimming difficult, even impossible.

In fact, curly coats are common in water dogs, as they are so effective at repelling water and insulating their wearers. Other water dogs with curly coats include the Curly-Coated Retriever, the Portuguese Water Dog, and the American and Irish Water Spaniels.

Grooming a curly coat takes skills with scissors and a lot of practice.

Curly-coated breeds are perfect for people who either don't mind paying a groomer once a month to groom their pets, or for those who want to learn all about the art of grooming curly coats. If you love the look, you may appreciate your pet's curly coat even more if you learn to take care of it yourself.

Curly-Coated Breeds

American Water Spaniel	Irish Water Spaniel	Portuguese Water Dog
Bedlington Terrier	Kerry Blue Terrier	Puli
Bichon Frise	Komondor	
Curly-Coated Retriever	Poodle: Standard, Miniature, and Toy	

Defining Your Grooming Goals

Finally, no matter what coat type your dog may have, you have some choices to make about grooming. Certain aspects of grooming are non-negotiable to keep pets healthy: good hygiene, sound dental care, and nail clipping are among them. Other aspects depend on you, including:

• How much time you want to put into your dog's grooming;

• Whether your dog is a show dog (or whether you just want him to *look* like one);

• Whether your dog is a working dog (like a herding or gun dog) and needs a coat to help, not to hinder, his performance;

• Whether your dog is a performance dog in agility, obedience, flyball, or other dog sports, and needs coat to help, not to hinder, his performance;

• Whether your dog is a family pet and you don't care much about how he looks, as long as he is clean and comfortable.

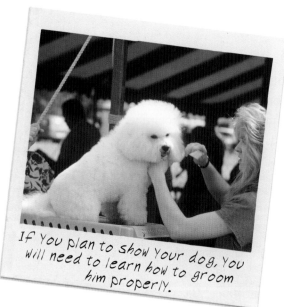

If you plan to show your dog, you will need to learn how to groom him properly.

Determining how you feel about grooming will affect your setup, your grooming schedule, and the tools and products you decide to use. A smooth-coated dog could require nothing more than a basic weekly brush-down for his coat, but if you want your dog to gleam like a show dog, you might also rub him down regularly with a curry brush, polish him with a square of velvet, and lightly spray him with an oil-based coat dressing to give him that extra gleam. Maybe you will keep your long-coated dog trimmed in a cute, tufty puppy cut for convenience and comfort, or maybe the two of you will enjoy a long and luxurious brushing session every day or two to keep that coat at its full, stunning length.

Before you move on to the next chapter, where you will learn about how to set up your in-home grooming station and what products and tools to buy, think about your grooming goals and what exactly you want for your dog. Throughout this book, you'll find lots of options, so you can choose between full-blown, all-out grooming glamour or short-cut, quick-and-easy grooming basics. When it comes to tools, you will find grooming essentials and grooming luxuries. How far you want to go with grooming is all up to you.

Once your goals are clearly defined, you'll be ready to establish a grooming routine that will keep your dog looking his best.

Part Two

Ready, Set, Groom!

"No, no, no! MY natural part is on the left!"

Getting Started

Ready for the nuts and bolts of grooming setup? It's time to get organized, set up a grooming station, plan your schedule, buy your supplies, and map out your grooming routine. Although some dogs will be fine if you brush them whenever you think about it and trim their nails when you notice they are getting a little too long, most dogs will benefit from a regular grooming routine in a comfortable environment, designed to suit their individual needs with the right equipment and supplies.

Every home groomer should have a comfortable, well-lit location for pet grooming, easily accessible supplies, and a good system for keeping records. In this chapter, you'll learn the

Every home groomer should have the proper supplies with which to groom his or her dog.

basics of a home grooming setup. Good grooming begins with good planning, and this chapter will help to get you started.

Design Your Plan

Grooming consists of two basic levels, which we will call Level I and Level II for the purpose of this book. Each level is a necessary part of your dog's grooming routine: Level I is for basic maintenance, and Level II includes a bath and a more thorough check, as well as clipping and styling of the coat.

Some people choose to do Level I grooming themselves, but leave Level II grooming to the professional groomer. Others enjoy learning how to do Level II grooming themselves. Let's look at what each level involves, so you can best incorporate all necessary grooming steps into your routine.

There are lots of things you can do yourself to keep your dog well groomed.

Level I Grooming

Grooming Level I is the kind of grooming you do every few days to keep your dog in good shape: brushing, combing, checking the body for changes, cleaning teeth, and perhaps clipping off toenail tips. While some people do this kind of maintenance once a week or even less often, a daily grooming session is a pleasant and effective way to bond with your pet. No, your dog's coat might not need to be brushed every day, but that doesn't mean you *can't* brush it every day, and every pet will benefit from a little pampering on a daily basis. (Wouldn't we all?)

Level I grooming generally consists of the following steps (although you can certainly alter these to fit your individual pet and situation).

• Coat massage to stimulate skin and to check for lumps, bumps, sores, rashes, and other skin changes;

• All-over brushing;

• Quick run-through with a comb to check for fleas and any missed tangles;

• Ear check;

• Eye check;

• Wipe down face and eyes with a moist, clean cloth and apply eye drops if necessary (for breeds with tendency towards dry eyes);

• Brush or wipe down teeth;

• Check and handle each paw, clipping off toenail tips if necessary;

• A notation in your grooming journal about what you did and how your pet looks and acts today (see the last section in this chapter for more on your grooming journal);

• A treat for being *such* a good dog!

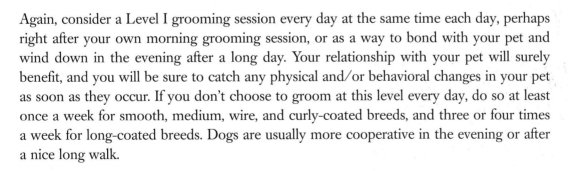

The time you spend grooming your dog can help to build the bond between you.

Again, consider a Level I grooming session every day at the same time each day, perhaps right after your own morning grooming session, or as a way to bond with your pet and wind down in the evening after a long day. Your relationship with your pet will surely benefit, and you will be sure to catch any physical and/or behavioral changes in your pet as soon as they occur. If you don't choose to groom at this level every day, do so at least once a week for smooth, medium, wire, and curly-coated breeds, and three or four times a week for long-coated breeds. Dogs are usually more cooperative in the evening or after a nice long walk.

Level II Grooming
Level II grooming is the kind of grooming pets need every few months. For long-coated, curly-coated, wire-haired, and medium-coated breeds in full show coats, Level II grooming

is best done every four to six weeks. For smooth-coated dogs, Level II grooming every two months is fine, with a bath even less often. A Level II grooming session usually consists of the following steps (again, vary these according to the needs of your pet and your situation).

• More thorough check of skin, eyes, ears, teeth, rear, paws, and pawpads;

• Parasite check and pesticide application when necessary;

• A thorough brush-out with tangle and mat removal;

• A thorough comb-out to ensure all tangles and mats are out of the coat;

• A bath and coat conditioning treatment;

• Nail clipping;

• Application of eye drops, ear powder, tooth scaling, and anal gland expressing, as necessary;

• Clipping and styling coat, as appropriate for breed.

If you choose to take your dog to a professional groomer for this level of grooming because you don't want to do the bathing, clipping, and styling yourself, that's fine. Professional groomers are widely available, and some have even hit the road in mobile grooming vans that will come to your house and groom your pet right in your own driveway. Or, you may find you enjoy grooming your dog so much that you would like to become a professional groomer yourself. To learn more about this fun and flexible career, check out the last section of this book.

Your dog's ears should be kept clean, dry, and free of waxy buildup.

Don't Just Pencil It In

Dogs thrive on routine, and even the most easygoing of dogs may be thrown off by sporadic grooming. "Uh-oh, is she or isn't she going for those nail trimmers! Run away! Run away!" However, dogs who learn that grooming is a weekly, or even a daily, part of the schedule will accept it more readily, and many look forward to it as a special time to spend with their owners. ("Hey, that brushing feels pretty good! Don't stop!")

Making grooming a habit is your responsibility and your challenge. Commit to grooming the same way you commit to brushing your teeth or paying your bills, and it will soon become a regular part of your routine. Whether your regular grooming sessions (brushing, combing, eyes, ears, and teeth) happen daily or weekly, schedule your sessions and allow a monthly longer session (for example, the first or last Sunday of each month) for bathing and more detailed attention to your pet's grooming needs. You are responsible for the dog's health and well-being. Remember that grooming is an important part of owning a dog.

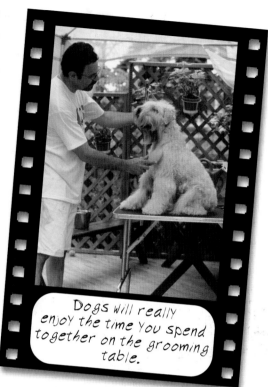

Dogs will really enjoy the time you spend together on the grooming table.

Part 2

Brush That Puppy!

Although some dogs balk at having nails trimmed, teeth brushed, or coat combed, dogs trained from puppyhood that grooming is part of the regular routine are a dream to groom. They have learned that good grooming is a part of life, and they would never think to argue about it! Diligent pet owners will soon discover that a dog accustomed to regular grooming is much better behaved for veterinary examinations, too. Begin with two- to three-minute grooming sessions and gradually build up the time in small increments. For a puppy, give a treat while each foot is being handled. Always give the treats while the dog is in the grooming location so they associate something good with each session. The treats can be something special, like a Nylabone®, or for puppies at risk for too-quick weight gain, they can be part of the dog's food portion for the day.

Set up a workable station when grooming your dog.

Table It

A grooming table is a valuable tool for a professional groomer, but home groomers may also find grooming much easier if they use one. Standard grooming tables are approximately 2 feet by 3 feet, but smaller tables are also available for toy breeds. Grooming tables have non-skid surfaces, and many come with grooming posts or arms, so dogs can be secured to a leash, and for larger dogs, a belly band. These posts keep dogs feeling secure and protect against escape before the dog is used to staying put for grooming. Grooming tables generally sell for less than a few hundred dollars for basic models, and some run under one hundred dollars.

Setting Up Your Grooming Station

The grooming station is the heart of your grooming routine. If you don't have a good place to groom your dog, you probably won't bother until grooming has become an emergency. A workable grooming station can be as simple or as elaborate as you want to make it. You can transform a spare room into a grooming center, or groom on the deck or porch where hair can fly without necessitating clean-up. You can invest in a grooming table, or groom on the counter (for a small dog) or on the floor (for a large dog) of your bathroom. You can also use a non-skid bathmat on top of a washer or dryer. It doesn't matter where you groom, as long as you have a station that makes grooming easy.

Location, Location, Location

Finding a good place to groom your dog can make all the difference in actually establishing the habit. A location for grooming that is convenient and pleasant will be conducive to the regular practice of grooming your dog. Where will you be most likely to groom your dog regularly? There are some questions to consider.

How much clean-up will your dog require? The mess your grooming sessions will make can determine where to groom. For example, long-haired dogs whose coat stays in the comb are easy to groom indoors, but brushing your short-coated shedder may release tiny hairs into the air, so you may prefer an outdoor location.

A harsh climate makes outdoor grooming inconvenient during much of the year; a temperate climate is more conducive to outdoor grooming.

That spare room or basement might be a great grooming studio, unless it is stuffy, uncomfortable, dim, or you have to make an extra trip up or downstairs that you probably won't be willing to make.

The ideal grooming location has plenty of lighting, is big enough to move around in, and is easy to clean. Whether you use a corner of your bathroom or the front step, choose a location and use it every time. Your dog will soon associate that location with grooming and will be comfortable and secure in knowing exactly what is going to happen in that spot. Sticking with one grooming location will make grooming easier on everyone.

Organization

Once you've secured a location, it's time to organize your grooming station. If grooming is a well-organized affair, it will be a pleasure, but if you have to spend 20 minutes looking for that brush—and where did you put those nail clippers?—you may be less inclined to bother.

If you have a small dog, you will need a raised surface on which to groom. Stooping down for half an hour to comb out your Shih Tzu is uncomfortable and hardly ergonomic. A grooming table can be a wonderful piece of equipment if you have space for it and choose to invest in one. Grooming tables put dogs at a comfortable grooming height and are covered in a non-skid surface so your dog can stand comfortably and safely. Or, put your toy dog on a bathroom counter on a towel or bathmat. A larger dog can stand on the floor as you sit on a stool or chair. Try different setups until you find one that is comfortable for you and your dog.

If you plan to do a lot of home grooming, a grooming table is a wise investment.

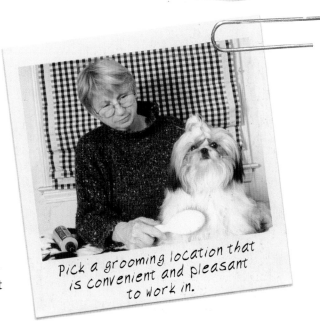

Pick a grooming location that is convenient and pleasant to work in.

Part 2

Organize your grooming equipment so everything is easy to find and use.

Next, organize your tools: brush, comb, clippers, and whatever else you will need for your dog (see the next section for notes on tool selection). Put them in a basket or set of baskets, or organize them in a container made to organize office or other tools. Keep in mind that you should be able to see what you need so you can reach it easily.

Finally, store the tools in a convenient location: a cabinet, a counter, or anywhere with easy access to your grooming area. If seeing the grooming tools will help you remember to groom, place them in plain sight. If clutter bugs you, stash them away, but be sure they are easy to get to when you need them.

Tools

Finally, you will need certain tools to groom your pet, and what kind of tools you need depends on what kind of pet you have. All dogs have certain supplies and equipment in common, but long coats require different grooming tools than smooth coats, wire coats, curly coats, etc.

Later in this book, as we talk about grooming different coat types, we'll talk more about the individual tools you will need for certain coat types, but to get you started, the following is a list of the tools you will need for grooming.

For All Breeds and Coat Types
• Natural bristle brush

• Combination medium/fine-toothed comb

• Small curved and/or blunt-tipped scissors, for whisker and foot trimming

• Nail trimmers of appropriate size, made for use on dogs

• Nail file for smoothing rough nails

Join the Club

Every purebred dog recognized by the American Kennel Club (AKC), and many that aren't, have national breed clubs devoted to the preservation of that breed. National breed clubs are excellent sources of information about the dogs they champion. They can refer you to member breeders who promise to follow that breed club's code of ethics. They can provide information about the breed's look, temperament, best home, and proper care. Breed fanciers who want to be more involved can join the breed club, but their resources are also available to non-members.

Many of these breed clubs also publish free or low-cost grooming guides to help both novice and professional groomers understand how that individual breed should be groomed properly. Many national breed clubs post grooming information on their websites, along with who to contact for help and how to find breeders in your area. To locate contact information for your breed's national breed club, contact the AKC, or search your breed's name plus the term "breed clubs" on the internet. To contact the American Kennel Club, visit their web page at www.akc.org, or use their email contact form, where your email will be directed to the right department, at www.akc.org/akc/contact_akc.cfm. Or, call or write:

American Kennel Club

Public Education
5580 Centerview Drive
Raleigh, NC 27606

phone: (919) 816-3718
fax: (919) 816-4275
e-mail: publiced@akc.org
www.akc.org

Part 2

Optional Tools

These tools are for grooming beyond what is necessary for a pet. If you want to groom a show dog, or just want to groom precisely according to the grooming protocol for a show dog, you might also want to invest in the following.

• Thinning shears

• Terrier mitt (for terriers)

• Ear forceps for removing ear hair

• Nail grinder/dremel tool for filing nails

There are certain grooming tools that can be useful on any coat type.

Part 2

Clipper Tips

So many clippers—how do you choose which to use for your home grooming? Some clippers are labeled for pet use, but heavy-duty professional clippers don't cost much more and, with proper care, they will last for years. Professional clippers also come with a variety of detachable blades and combs. Cordless clippers are convenient if you want to groom in an area without an easily accessible outlet. Care for your clippers by cleaning after each use, and lubricating with clipper oil according to manufacturer's instructions.

A blow-dryer can be an excellent addition to your grooming equipment.

• Showerhead hose attachment, for easier bathing

• Grooming table

• Non-skid rubber mat for bathing and grooming

For Smooth Coats

Grooming the smooth-coated dog centers around good health, a shiny coat, and the accentuation of the breed's unique silhouette. Invest in the following:

• Rubber curry brush

• Hound glove

• Clippers with #10 blade for occasional neatening, depending on breed

• Chamois, flannel, silk, or velvet squares for polishing

• Blow-dryer with cool setting (optional, but good for small, easily chilled breeds like Chihuahuas and Italian Greyhounds)

For Medium Coats

Grooming the medium-coated dog is easy, as most medium-coated breeds are supposed to appear naturally without alteration. Brush, trim nails, clean ears, trim hair on feet and ears, and you're done! Invest in the following:

• Pin brush

• Coat rake

• Hound glove

• Shedding comb

• Rubber curry brush

• Blow-dryer with cool setting

Long Coats

Grooming the long-coated dog is largely centered around coat care and detangling. Invest in the following:

• Pin brush

• Slicker brush

• Shedding comb

• Wide-toothed comb for thickly coated breeds (such as Collies and Samoyeds)

• Mat comb

• Mat splitter

• Scissors, for shaping and trimming

• Clippers with a variety of blade sizes as relevant for breed (some long-coated breeds require clipping, others don't)

• Blow-dryer with cool setting

• Rubber bands, bows, ribbons, barrettes, etc., for those long-coated dogs with topknots

Wire Coats

Grooming the wire coat requires brushing and

Brush-Off

Keep your brushes and combs in good condition. When bristles begin to bend, pins fall out, or comb teeth break off, replace your tools, or you could risk damaging your dog's coat and even his skin.

There are several types of brushes that can be used on medium- to long-coated dogs.

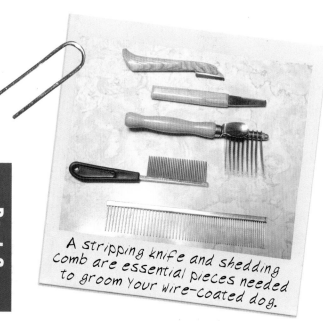

A stripping knife and shedding comb are essential pieces needed to groom your wire-coated dog.

Scissors are necessary for shaping and trimming the coat.

plucking or stripping to remove dead hairs, keeping the coat healthy and bright. Invest in the following:

• Natural bristle brush

• Slicker brush

• Hound glove

• Combination medium/fine-toothed comb

• Shedding comb

• Stripping knife

• Scissors, for shaping and trimming

• Electric clippers with a variety of blade sizes as relevant for breed, for shaping and keeping anal area clean

• Blow-dryer with cool setting.

Curly Coats

For crisp, marcelled curls, never brush that curly coat after a bath! Wash, condition, shape, and dry. Some curly coats with a more powder-puff appearance are brushed and combed, so technique depends on your breed's particular look and clip.

• Natural bristle brush

• Slicker brush

• Pin brush

• Coat rake

• Combination medium/fine-toothed metal comb

• Shedding comb

• Scissors, for shaping and trimming

• Electric clippers with a variety of blade sizes as relevant for breed, for shaping and keeping anal area clean.

Products

Although you can customize your product selection to your breed and to those products you want to use, this is a general list of the kinds of products you will want to consider for stocking your grooming station. The products listed as necessary form the basis of good grooming. Optional products are for those home groomers who want to go the extra mile.

Necessary Products

• Shampoo for your dog's coat type

• Coat conditioner for your dog's coat type

• Petroleum jelly to protect eyes and ears

• Nail coagulant or styptic pencil

• Medicated ear powder or other ear cleaning liquid, such as rubbing alcohol or a product designed for this purpose

• Eye drops for moistening and cleaning eyes

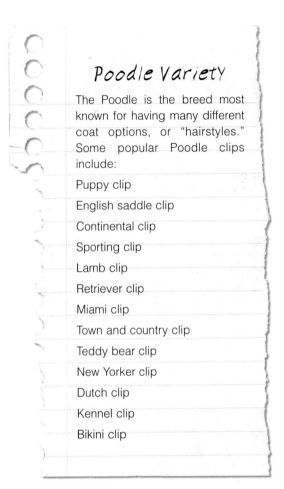

Poodle Variety

The Poodle is the breed most known for having many different coat options, or "hairstyles." Some popular Poodle clips include:

Puppy clip

English saddle clip

Continental clip

Sporting clip

Lamb clip

Retriever clip

Miami clip

Town and country clip

Teddy bear clip

New Yorker clip

Dutch clip

Kennel clip

Bikini clip

Part 2

A NYlabone® is a safe reward for a grooming session.

• Cotton balls

• Cotton swabs.

Optional Products
• Talcum powder, for keeping skin wrinkles dry

• Lanolin or oil-based coat spray, for sheen

• Mineral oil for polishing nails

• Cologne or other scented coat spray.

The Grooming Journal
The last aspect of grooming preparation is to establish a grooming journal. The grooming journal will become an invaluable record of your pet's health. In it, you can record what you do at each grooming session, as well as keep a record of each vet visit, changes in your dog's habits and behavior, what you feed your dog, how much your dog eats and drinks each day, and anything you notice during grooming sessions: sensitive areas, lumps, bumps, rashes, sores, coat changes, dental changes, etc.

Depending on how much time you spend on your grooming journal, you can also devote space to recording funny stories about the things your pet does each day. Include photos of your pet, from puppyhood through the senior years. Always bring your grooming journal to the vet with you so you can write down all tests, shots, advice, and suggested vaccination schedules you may forget. Let your grooming journal be a record of your pet's life, and you may be surprised how often you refer to it.

A journal can help keep track of your dog's health.

Your Grooming Journal

Design your grooming journal in a way that works for you. Or, use or modify this template to help you keep track of your grooming sessions:

DATE:

GROOMING PROCEDURES:

PHYSICAL NOTES:

BEHAVIORAL NOTES:

Choose a sturdy book with plenty of pages. Organize your journal in whatever way works for you. Maybe you prefer a binder with sections for grooming dates/notes, veterinary information, diet, and behavior notes. Maybe a bound book with blank pages is more your style, or perhaps you will keep a journal on your computer.

Now you're ready to start grooming. The next section of this book will take you through the basics of actually grooming your pet, from brush-out and bath to the finishing touches.

The Pre-Bath Brush-Out

In this next section of the book, we will take you through the initial steps involved in the Level II grooming session: the thorough brush-out, the bath, and the finishing touches on your dog (Part Three of this book will look at clipping, trimming, and styling, as well as more detailed advice on caring for individual coat types).

The heart and soul of your Level II grooming session is the brush-out. Brushing is indeed at the very core of grooming. No matter what coat type your dog has, brushing and combing every few days will keep shedding to a minimum, stimulate the skin, and keep the coat shiny and healthy. A neglected coat is a coat that is never brushed, but

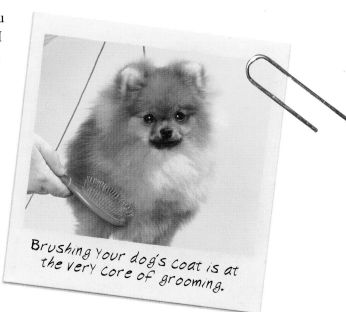

Brushing your dog's coat is at the very core of grooming.

Part 2

Make sure to brush your dog's coat thoroughly before bathing him.

a frequently brushed coat is a joy to behold, whether worn by a Labrador Retriever or a Lhasa Apso.

But before a bath, grooming is particularly important. Water will tighten and worsen mats and tangles, so this pre-bath brush-out is essential for removing mats. Even in dogs with shorter coats, a pre-bath brush-out will remove shed coat, loosen dead skin, distribute natural oils, and prepare the coat so bathing will be most effective. Use a spray bottle with water or coat conditioner to keep the coat slightly damp while brushing and combing. This also helps eliminate static electricity.

Ready Your Tools

You will use most of your grooming tools during the brush-out, according to your dog's coat type: your natural bristle brush, pin brush, slicker brush, comb, mat comb, hound glove, and/or any other brush you may require for your breed. Review the notes on which brushes and combs your breed's coat type requires, to be sure you have the tools you need.

Many brushes and combs can substitute for other types, especially if you are not grooming for the show ring. A pin brush can take the place of a slicker brush in some breeds. A hound glove can take the place of a curry comb. However, to best use each tool for its specific purpose, the following is a brief description of what each kind of brush and comb is really meant to do.

• Natural bristle brush: This brush has bristles that are softer, gentler, and less likely to cause static

Seasonal Coat Care

Seasonal coat care is an important consideration for dogs that spend a lot of time outdoors. Coats should be washed, or at least rinsed, after summer dips in natural lakes, ponds, puddles, and any form of saltwater. Coats require more brushing and attention after long summer days in the field, on a hike, or romping in the park or yard. Brush out burrs, pests, and dirt every day. In winter, keep coats clean and dry so dogs don't become chilled and keep paws cleaned of salt and other de-icing chemicals your dog may encounter during walks.

electricity in a dog's coat than artificial bristles such as those made from nylon. Natural bristle brushes are all-purpose brushes designed to smooth hair and distribute natural oils to the coat.

• Pin brush: Pin brushes are generally used for long-haired breeds like Shih Tzu and Lhasa Apso, and heavily double-coated breeds like Old English Sheepdogs and Chow Chows. Pin brushes help to detangle long, tangle-prone coats and also work well on hard wire coats for an overall brushing prior to hand stripping.

• Slicker brush: The slicker brush has densely set wire teeth effective at removing mats and dead coat from long-, wire-, and curly-coated dogs. Slicker brushes are great when your dog is blowing coat because they efficiently remove large amounts of dead hair, but because they can also pull out some of the live hair, they aren't ideal for show dogs who want to maintain luxurious coats. They are ideal for grooming heavy shedders around the house, however, as they get rid of maximum amounts of hair with minimum effort.

• Rubber curry brush: These oval-shaped rubber brushes are perfect for smooth coats because they polish the coat and remove dead hair, minimizing shedding, but the rounded rubber "bristles" are gentle on the sensitive skin of smooth-coated breeds.

• Fine/medium/wide-toothed combs: Fine and medium combs are best for dogs with soft, silky, fine- to medium-textured hair. They work through the coat to remove any last traces of tangle, and they also double as

A pin brush is generally used for long-haired breeds to help detangle the coat.

Combs are best used on dogs with short or fine-textured coats.

A quick brushing to remove dead hair and distribute oils will leave your hound's coat healthy and shiny.

Brushing for Parasite Control

Even the most well-groomed show dog can pick up fleas and ticks at an outdoor dog show, but a well-brushed dog with healthy skin and a tangle-free coat will be easier to treat for parasites, and regular brushing and combing will help you spot any pests right away so you can take action to prevent a flea infestation. Talk to your vet about the best methods for flea control for your dog, and never remove a tick with your bare hands. A burst tick contains bacteria and could infect you. Use a tissue, rubber gloves, and/or a special instrument such as tweezers designed for removing ticks.

flea combs to help remove parasites and flea dirt when present. Wide-toothed combs are better for breeds with very thick, dense coats, but they serve the same purpose: to remove all tangles after brushing. Combs should feel comfortable in your hand, and metal combs with rounded teeth are sturdy and gentle on skin. In dogs prone to static electricity, try a wooden comb.

• Mat comb/mat splitter/coat rake: These "combs" are specifically designed to remove mats in long and curly coats. These tools break up matted hair with angled teeth and work best in conjunction with a spray or liquid detangling product. Later in the book, there is a more detailed discussion of how to get rid of mats.

• Hound glove: These gloves actually slip over your hand. They are covered on one side with natural bristles. Rub these gloves over your smooth-coated dog to remove dead hair efficiently, brightening and shining the coat.

Choose the tools that you need for your individual breed (for more on how to groom your dog's individual coat type, see Part Three of this book), and let's get brushing!

Brushing Procedures

Brushing out your dog before a bath can be time-consuming or quick, depending on coat type and condition. Although it doesn't really matter which parts of your dog you brush in what order (as long as you cover the whole coat), an orderly and systematic brush-out from front to back and bottom to top will ensure that you cover all parts of your dog. It will also reassure your dog that you will always groom the same way, so he knows exactly what to expect.

In long-coated dogs and long curly-coated dogs especially, brushing (and combing) takes a long time and a lot of patience. Having a routine can be reassuring to your dog, especially before she is entirely accustomed to the process. Brush and then comb each section before moving on to the next section. In dogs with smooth coats, brushing is sufficient unless you are combing through the coat to remove fleas.

Feel free to vary this order, but try to stay consistent. Many groomers find that brush-outs work best if they follow this sequence. Call it your 12-step grooming program.

Back Legs

First, begin at your dog's back legs. Brush down each leg with a natural bristle brush for smooth and medium coats, and a pin brush or slicker brush for long, wire, and curly coats. If you come to tangles or mats, hold the hair at the root as you work out the tangle with the slicker brush or with a mat comb (later in this book there are specific instructions on using a mat comb to remove a mat from a long coat). Holding the hair above the tangle will minimize discomfort to your dog because you won't be yanking at the skin.

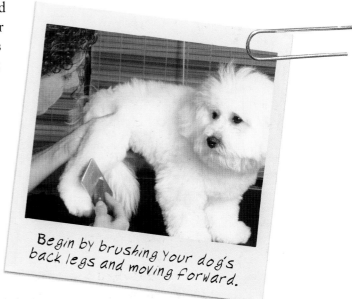

Begin by brushing your dog's back legs and moving forward.

Once the back legs are completely free of tangles and mats, finish with a comb. The comb should run smoothly through the hair from root to end. In smooth coats, a comb can ensure that your dog is parasite-free even

Work from the top of each leg to the bottom; first brushing, then removing any tangles or mats.

Brush out your dog's tail from base to tip, covering top, sides, and bottom.

if it is unnecessary as a tangle monitor. Don't worry about trimming paw hair or nails just yet. You can put these finishing touches on your dog after the bath.

Front Legs

Next, move to the front legs. Again, work from the top of each leg to the bottom, first brushing the coat, then removing tangles and mats one at a time, then working through the coat a final time with a comb.

Tail

Back to the rear again, brush out your dog's tail (if he has one) from base to tip, covering top, sides, and bottom. Even a smooth-coated tail can use a good brushing to remove dead hair, but many breeds have a feathered tail, and this must be kept brushed and combed to stay mat-free, especially at the base, where hair can tangle against the rear end. If your dog doesn't have a tail or has a short, docked tail, brush what is there.

Hindquarters

After brushing the tail, turn your attention to your dog's hindquarters. Many breeds have thicker furnishings in the hindquarter area. Brush out feathers, "pantaloons," or the smooth haunches of your dog, slowly working out tangles in long coats. When cutting a tangle, cut in the direction the hair grows, and split the tangle with the scissors. Then use a brush or comb to work the tangle free.

Brush carefully around the anal area, checking for mats and ensuring your dog's rear end is clean and free of soil. Be careful not to brush over sensitive skin. Using a blunt-tipped scissors, trim off any tangles that are unworkable and any soil stuck in long hair. For extra cleanliness, shave just around the anal area with a clipper (but never directly over the anal area), or trim closely with a blunt-tipped scissors.

Finally, comb the hindquarters to check one more time that this area is tangle-free.

Back

Next, brush down your dog's back, from nape to tail base. Or, in long-coated dogs, begin at the base of the tail and work through sections of hair, brushing out tangles and mats as you go. Follow with a comb on each section until the entire back is tangle-free.

Sides

Brush your dog along each side from nape to tail base. Again, in long-coated dogs, begin at the base of the tail and work through sections of hair. In dogs with shorter coats, you can brush the back and sides together with long, firm strokes to stimulate skin and distribute natural oils to the coat.

Belly

Now it's time to do your dog's underside. In many dogs, the belly has little hair, but check it over and brush lightly to avoid brush burn on your dog's sensitive underside. Don't brush areas without hair or with more skin showing than hair.

Chest

With your dog in a "sit" position, brush the chest, working out tangles.

Brush down your dog's back from nape to tail base and follow with a comb to ensure he is tangle-free.

Brush your dog's belly lightly to avoid hurting his sensitive underside.

Part 2

If your dog has long ears, spend extra time brushing.

Part 2

Neck

Many dogs have longer, thicker coats around the neck area, called a "ruff" in some breeds. Get all the way down to the skin with the brush and then with the comb to make sure no hidden tangles remain in the undercoat of the ruff.

Ears

If your dog has long ear hair, spend time brushing and combing ears carefully and gently. Beautifully combed ears make a big difference in the overall appearance of a long-haired dog (or a long-ear-haired dog!). Work out tangles gently, as many dogs have sensitive ears.

Oh, Those Ears!

Breeds that need special attention to the long hair on their ears include:

Afghan Hound	English Springer Spaniel	Petit Basset Griffon Vendeen (PBGV)
American Water Spaniel	English Toy Spaniel	Polish Lowland Sheepdog
Bearded Collie	Field Spaniel	Poodle (all sizes)
Bedlington Terrier	Gordon Setter	Portugese Water Dog
Bernese Mountain Dog	Irish Setter	Puli
Bichon Frise	Irish Water Spaniel	Saluki
Briard	Japanese Chin	Shih Tzu
Cavalier King Charles Spaniel	Lhasa Apso	Skye Terrier
Chinese Crested	Löwchen	Sussex Spaniel
Cocker Spaniel	Maltese	Tibetan Terrier
Dachshund (longhaired)	Old English Sheepdog	Yorkshire Terrier
Dandie Dinmont Terrier	Otterhound	
English Cocker Spaniel	Papillon	
English Setter	Pekingese	

Give a Kid a Brush

Kids love dogs, and involving your kids in daily grooming is a great way to foster this relationship, teaching kids that dogs need care, and teaching dogs that kids can care *for* them, gently and responsibly. When your child is old enough to follow directions and be gentle (this could be anywhere from age 4 to age 12, depending on your child's personality), teach your child how to use brushes and combs on your dog's coat. Always supervise grooming sessions!

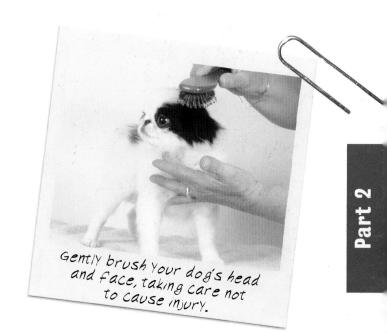

Gently brush your dog's head and face, taking care not to cause injury.

Head

Gently brush your dog's head and finish with a comb. In smooth-coated dogs, a rub down with a hound glove is enough.

Face

If your dog has long facial hair, brush and comb it carefully, trimming as necessary and appropriate for your breed. In smooth-coated dogs, simply wipe down the face with a moist, soft cloth.

Brushed and Ready

Finally, your dog is tangle-free and ready for a bath. Easy, right? Not necessarily! Bathing your dog correctly is an art. Read on for more information on how to give your dog the ultimate shampoo.

If your dog has long facial hair, brush it gently in the manner and style that distinguishes the breed.

The Bath

Giving a dog a bath can be as simple as rinsing him down in a child's swimming pool in the backyard during the summer, or as complex as a full-blown spa ritual, complete with bathing harness and a bevy of fancy coat products designed to whiten, darken, brighten, de-tangle, shine, and leave your dog with a designer aroma to rival a fancy French perfume. However, there are many ways to make bathing easier, and many ways in which bathing makes subsequent grooming sessions easier, too. In this chapter, we'll show you how to give your dog a bath that makes a difference—one that will facilitate grooming and be easy and as pleasant as possible for your dog.

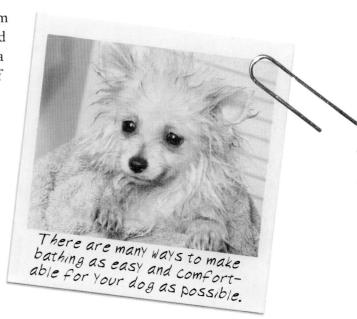

There are many ways to make bathing as easy and comfortable for your dog as possible.

Bath Inventory

Once your dog is completely brushed, combed, and tangle-free, he is ready for a bath. Now you must get ready, too, and that means preparing all the necessary equipment and supplies so that you can reach what you need when you need it. If you put that dog in the bathtub under running water and then have to go in search of shampoo or a scrub brush, we all know what will happen: a jump, a shake, and you will be a left with a soaked bathroom and a wet dog bounding around the house.

To wash your dog, you will need some basic supplies:

• Shampoo

• Conditioner

• A sponge

• A scrub brush

• A small scrub brush or soft-bristled nail brush (for the face)

• A bath mat

• A hand-held sprayer or a large plastic cup for rinsing

• A plastic or rubber apron for you (or, wear clothes that can get wet–some precautionary pet owners don a bathing suit for this job)

• A nylon collar and leash, if you think your dog is likely to bolt or will be difficult to hang on to in the bath

• A heavy towel (or two)

Assemble your supplies, then place them within easy reach of the sink or tub where you will bathe your dog.

Something Stinks

If your dog gets into something really stinky, such as a tangle with a skunk or a roll in a dead animal's remains, you may have to take some extra measures. Many pet stores sell de-skunking preparations, or try the old-fashioned remedy: a few cans of tomato juice poured over the coat and allowed to sit for a few minutes. Rinse well and repeat. (Warning: This process can turn white coats pink.) You can also mix a quart of hydrogen peroxide, a quarter-cup baking soda, and a dash of shampoo. Multiple shampoos may also be in order.

Part 2

Choosing a Shampoo

With so many shampoos on the market, it's not easy to decide which to use. Yet, for most breeds, a basic, all-purpose shampoo is fine. If you want your shampoo to do more than clean, you might also consider a specialty shampoo.

You can choose a shampoo that will accentuate your dog's coat color.

• Accentuate your dog's coat color by choosing a shampoo made for white, black, or red coats.

• Shampoos designed to deliver extra conditioning to long or curly coats can make post-bath grooming even easier.

• For wire-coated dogs, look for a shampoo designed to preserve the crisp texture of your dog's coat.

• Many dogs have sensitive skin or eyes. A hypoallergenic shampoo can minimize sensitivity reactions to bathing.

• If your dog already has a rash, allergies, itching, or other sensitive skin conditions, look for a medicated shampoo designed to treat your dog's problem (your vet should be able to recommend a good medicated shampoo for your dog).

• Flea season? Consider a shampoo containing a gentle anti-flea ingredient such as pyrethrin or limonene, or any of several natural botanicals designed to repel fleas, such as neem oil.

• Sensitive eyes? Consider a tearless shampoo.

Size Matters

But where will you bathe your dog? First, consider your dog's size. While you can bathe a Yorkie in a clean kitchen sink, your Labrador Retriever isn't going to fit. Your Great Dane may outsize your bathtub, but your Chihuahua might be hard to hold on to all the way down in that big tub.

Size matters when it comes to bathing, and so does coat type. Long and curly coats needs more time and attention in the bath, and if you are stooping or kneeling uncomfortably, you may not be able to spend as much time as you should washing and conditioning your dog's coat.

Bathing Toy Breeds

In general, consider bathing toy dogs in a kitchen or bathroom sink. If your sink doesn't come equipped with a drain that will trap hair, purchase a simple, inexpensive one that sits over the drain. Make sure the sink is clean and the counter space is free. You don't want to try to bathe a dog amidst piles of dirty dishes!

Kitchen sinks are good for bathing small dogs, especially when they come equipped with sprayers, because dogs are easy to reach and easy to rinse. If you keep both your kitchen and your dog squeaky-clean, you won't have to worry about contaminating your food preparation area. Just spray with a disinfectant and wipe down counters and sink when you are done. Plus, you'll have a better time holding onto your small dog if you don't have to kneel on a hard tile floor.

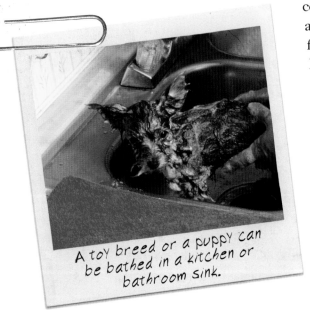

A toy breed or a puppy can be bathed in a kitchen or bathroom sink.

If you can't quite get yourself to bathe your dog in your kitchen, consider the bathroom sink basin or the laundry tub. You can always purchase a spray attachment. Some bathroom sinks have faucets that aren't compatible with sprayers, and if yours isn't, look for one with a long enough hose that you can attach it to the bathtub faucet or showerhead and stretch it over to the sink.

Bathing Medium-Sized Breeds

Medium-sized breeds are too big for a kitchen sink, but fit nicely in your bathtub or a laundry tub. Dogs from approximately 15 to 50 pounds are easy to bathe in a regular bathtub. Fold a towel on the floor to make kneeling more comfortable. Invest in a good sprayer, and put a bath mat on the tub floor so your dog doesn't slip and slide. A hose diverter for the shower connection can be installed between the showerhead and pipe and will make bathing much easier.

If kneeling beside the tub is a problem, booster tubs can be purchased at a reasonable price. Water hook-ups and drainage can be near a bathtub or laundry area.

Bathing Large Breeds

You can bathe large breeds in your bathtub or shower, too, but if your dog is large enough to step in and out of the bathtub without blinking an eye, remember that a good shake of that coat will spray water far and wide. This can be avoided by stepping into the shower with your dog and closing the shower curtain. Some pet owners like to bathe their larger dogs outside in a child's swimming pool or other large basin, or simply by using the garden hose, if your dog doesn't mind the cold water.

Step-By-Step Bathing Guide

You have your location, you have your supplies, and you are properly suited up for the likelihood of getting wet. Now it's time to transform that nicely brushed and combed dog into a squeaky *clean* dog.

If your dog isn't yet trained to stand nicely for bathing, put a nylon, plain buckle collar on him and attach a nylon leash. Loop this around a secure fixture, such as a shower railing, or attach the leash to your belt or wrist. Tub restraints with suction cups work well for holding smaller breeds. Once your dog is used to bathing, you may not have to do this, but some dogs will always try to escape the water, and some kind of precautionary restraint may necessarily become a part of the bathing routine. A leash and collar can actually make your dog feel more secure in the bathtub

If the weather is warm, it may be easier to bathe your larger breed outside.

Hosed!

Always test the water coming out of the garden hose before spraying it on your dog. Water sitting in a hose in the sun can become extremely hot, and you could risk scalding your dog if you don't let this hot water run out of the hose first. Also, if the water is very cold, your dog may be less inclined to enjoy his bath. If the water coming out of your garden hose isn't a good temperature for bathing, consider washing your dog inside the house and letting him dry off in the warm sun.

Begin bathing your dog by thoroughly wetting his entire coat.

and your dog may prefer them. Very important: Do not use any kind of choke collar or any material that will swell when wet to restrain the dog when bathing!

Bathing your dog in the same sequence each time can also make the bath experience more comfortable, because he will know exactly what to expect. Try the following bathing sequence, then vary it according to your needs.

The Wet-Down

First, wet down your dog. Always test the water before applying it to your dog. Lukewarm water of approximately 110 degrees Fahrenheit is ideal. Depending on your dog's coat thickness and water-repellant qualities, this can take a few seconds, or a couple of minutes of heavy soaking. Double coats and curly coats tend to repel water. Make sure your dog is wet all the way down to the skin.

As with brushing, you can wet heavy, long coats according to a sequence. Start from the back and work your way to the front, saturating hindquarters, body, front, and then carefully, the head, avoiding the eyes and ear canal. Move slowly and talk encouragingly to your dog so he doesn't associate the experience with discomfort or fear.

The Soap-Up

Once your dog's coat is completely saturated, apply shampoo according to the directions. Generally, the more coat you have to cover, the more shampoo you will need. Grab that sponge and work the shampoo into a lather (or use your hands if you prefer–better exercise, but you may

Waterproofing

Well-behaved bathers won't struggle and probably won't get soap and water in their ears and eyes, but before you know for sure how well your dog will respond to a bath, protect those sensitive eyes and ears before getting your dog wet. Even a tear-free shampoo can irritate your dog's eyes, so put a drop of mineral oil in the corner of each eye to repel water. Also, protect your dog's ears from getting wet, as a damp ear canal can encourage infection. Dip two cotton balls in a little petroleum jelly and insert in each ear to protect the ear canal. You can also hold the ears flat against the head to prevent water in the ear canal.

generate less lather). Completely cover your dog with suds, except for the face, which you can do at the end.

Work It In

Now grab that brush and gently scrub the soap all the way to the skin, massaging the skin and distributing the shampoo evenly over the coat. You can also work that lather in with your fingers, allowing you to feel the dog's skin for any unusual lumps or bumps. Your dog will probably enjoy this part–it should feel great. Use your small brush or nail brush to gently suds-up your dog's ears and face, avoiding the eyes and ear canals.

Rinse It Out

Now, using your hand-held sprayer or plastic container, rinse your dog's coat of all signs of soap. Long, heavy, and double coats may take awhile. Keep rinsing until the rinse water runs completely clear. Even smooth coats may need to be rinsed a couple of times. Rinsing will probably

Massage the shampoo in the coat and distribute it evenly over the dog's body.

Lather, Rinse and Repeat?

If your dog is extremely dirty or got into something very smelly, you may need to lather, rinse, and then repeat. For most dogs, however, one lather-rinse cycle is plenty.

Make sure to rinse your dog's coat completely, removing all traces of shampoo.

take longer than sudsing. Soap left in your dog's coat can be a skin irritant and will compromise the look and feel of his coat. A dog's coat that is not rinsed properly will appear dull and flaky.

Condition
Next, apply a conditioner or cream rinse after rinsing shampoo from the coat. Follow the package directions and rinse well. A conditioner will keep hair soft and manageable, but may be overkill for smooth coats and could compromise the harsh texture of wire coats, so reserve conditioners/cream rinses for medium-, long-, and curly-coated breeds.

Dry
Finally, dry your dog's coat. Ring as much water out of the coat with your hands as you can, either by squeezing or by running your palm along the coat like a squeegee. Then, dry as much of your dog's coat as you can with a heavy towel.

Your dog will have the impulse to shake out his coat; however, try to dry him as much as possible with a heavy towel.

Wet dogs have an automatic impulse to shake, and even if you think you have dried your dog pretty well, you'll probably feel a fine spray when your dog shakes himself after you remove him from the tub or sink. After that efficient shake, smooth-coated dogs usually don't need any more drying, but you aren't finished with your grooming session, so don't let your dog bound along on her merry way just yet.

For thicker and longer-coated dogs, blow-drying will dry the coat more quickly, plus it will put it into good shape for clipping and styling, if appropriate for your breed. Use a cool or warm setting on your dog, constantly monitoring the blow-dryer temperature to make sure it doesn't get too hot.

For long or curly coats, blow-dry a section at a time, brushing or combing and fluffing lightly and quickly as you go, depending on coat type and desired appearance. For straight coats, dry quickly in sections to avoid kinks and waves, brushing out each section briskly to keep it smooth. If some

Drying the Dog

Whether you let your dog air dry or blow-dry partway, keep your dog inside until she is completely dry, especially if the weather is even a little brisk or breezy. Small dogs and sighthounds in particular don't like or tolerate getting chilled, and a wet coat can make your dog even more uncomfortable. And, although a hot sunny day is nice for drying a wet coat, many wet dogs love to roll around in the grass or (Oh no!) a nice dry patch of dirt to dry themselves off, so if your carpet is cleaner than your yard (let's hope it is!), let your dog dry indoors, if only to preserve his clean coat for a little bit longer.

Use a cool or warm setting when blow-drying your dog in order to avoid overdrying or burning the skin.

Part 2

parts of the coat dry too quickly and kink up, re-wet them and blow-dry straight. Some curly coats can benefit from a diffuser to keep the curl in the coat. Other curly coats should be brushed out, depending on the breed and style. (For more on blow-drying long and curly coats, see the appropriate chapters in Part Three.)

The Doggy Manicure

Take a look at those paws. Are your dog's nails neatly trimmed and short, or are they long, curving out from his paws and causing his paw pads to spread out when he steps? Nail trimming is essential not only for keeping feet neat but also for preserving correct mobility and, ultimately, orthopedic health. Your dog can't walk or run correctly and comfortably if his nails are too long.

Start Early, Trim Often

Some pet owners claim their pets absolutely *hate* nail trimming–that the process is a horrible struggle or virtually impossible. Some give up and take their pets to a groomer to do the job. But nail trimming doesn't have to be a bad experience for

Nail trimming not only keeps your dog's feet looking neat, but it also preserves his orthopedic health.

Begin trimming your puppy's nails the first week you bring him home.

DewClaw Clip

Some dogs retain their dewclaws: vestigial toes higher up on the leg with nails attached. These nails must also be clipped regularly, or they can grow so long that they curve back around and pierce the skin. Keep an eye—and the trimmers—on dewclaws if your dog didn't have them removed in puppyhood.

dog and human alike. Trimming your dog's nails is easy if he is well trained to tolerate the practice. Many dogs don't like it–some breeds more than others–but those dogs whose nails were trimmed every week or two from puppyhood usually don't bat an eye at the procedure.

You can begin trimming your new puppy's nails the very first week you bring him home. Handle your puppy's paw pads frequently and make it rewarding. Wiggle each nail and press on each paw pad, then always offer lots of praise, petting, and a treat. Do this every day for the first few months of your puppy's life in order to teach your puppy that when a human touches his feet, good things happen.

After a week of paw play, let your puppy investigate the nail trimmer in the presence of rewards. Let him sniff it. Don't just pull it out and start clipping, or you could scare your puppy. Once your puppy has had a chance to investigate the nail trimmers, take them in your hand, take your puppy's paw, and carefully clip off just the very tip of the nail. Immediately reward your puppy. If he responds well, try another nail, and reward again. (A pocketful of tiny pieces of cheese, treats, or kibble–no larger than a fingernail–works well for most puppies.)

Keep the process fun and always clip off just a tiny bit of nail. One slip, resulting in clipping the puppy's nail vein (or "quick") and you could set back nail trimming for months, because clipping the quick hurts, and the nail will bleed. Be careful. Keep handling your puppy's paws, clip nails weekly, continue to give treats, and your puppy will soon learn that nail trimming is something rewarding, not something uncomfortable or scary.

This type of early training will also teach your dog exactly what those nail trimmers are about and exactly what to

Part 2

expect. Just like anything else in your dog's life, routines, especially those routines that begin in puppyhood, become comforting and familiar. If a weekly toenail trim has always been part of your dog's life, the job should be an easy one.

Weekly? Does your dog really need a weekly toe trim? Weekly trims are especially good for dogs who are always on carpets or grass. Actually, a monthly toe trim would be perfectly appropriate for most dogs, but a month is about the longest most dog owners should wait before trimming nails. However, trimming weekly has some real benefits.

• Weekly toenail trims involve only the clip of the toenail's tip. Monthly trims require cutting off more nail.

• Weekly toenail trims encourage the quick–that vein that runs down each nail–to recede, so that you can clip nails shorter without risking the bleeding associated with accidentally clipping the quick.

• Weekly toenail trims are more routine than monthly toenail trims, so your dog will get used to them more quickly.

• Weekly toenail trims are so quick and easy that they are much less stressful on your pet. These short sessions, especially when followed by lots of praise and perhaps a tasty treat or Nylabone®, will quickly become pleasant and rewarding for your dog.

The Doggy Manicure, Step By Step

Nail trimming should be part of your monthly grooming routine. You can trim your dog's nails first,

Trimming your dog's toenails on a weekly basis has real benefits.

The Concrete Manicure

Dogs who are walked daily on hard surfaces or dogs who spend a lot of time on cement, stones, or other hard surfaces may not need their nails trimmed as often because the cement will naturally wear down the nail surface. Inside dogs and dogs who spend most of their time on grass or carpet will need more frequent nail trimming, however.

A nail grinder or a dremel can aid in caring for your dog's nails.

after brushing, or just after your dog has been washed and dried. Trimming nails after the bath may be the easiest, especially for large dogs with thick nails, because bathing helps to soften the nails.

First, prepare your tools.

• Nail trimmers

• Nail file or nail grinder/dremel tool

• A styptic pencil or styptic powder, silver nitrate stick, or other coagulant in case of bleeding

• Baby oil

• Treats (no larger than a fingernail)

Next, prepare your dog by having him sit on the grooming table or the ground in front of you, facing you. For larger dogs, have your dog stand on the floor. Stand or kneel next to your dog, facing the opposite direction, so you can lift up each paw behind the dog to clip it. (Stand or kneel on the right as you do the right paws, move to the left to do the left paws.)

Take one of your dog's paws gently in your left hand. Take the nail clipper in your right hand (or switch if you are left-handed). Hold the clipper blade parallel with the plane of your dog's paw and clip off the tip of the nail, just below the quick.

If your dog is comfortable lying on his back, you can sit on the floor and have the dog between your legs with the dog's head at your feet. This way the dog's

Take your dog's paw in your hands and clip off the tip of the nail, just above the quick.

Clipped Quick Fix

If your dog has light nails, you should be able to see the quick, the darker vein running down the middle of the nail. In dark-nailed dogs, you probably won't be able to see the quick and are best off clipping just the tip weekly. If you do clip the quick or grind down to it with an electric tool, your dog will feel pain and the quick will bleed, sometimes profusely. You'll need to stop the bleeding with the styptic pencil, styptic powder, silver nitrate stick, or other coagulant. Apply pressure and then the coagulant.

Clipping the quick, the vein running through your dog's nail, will cause bleeding, so be careful.

paw pads are facing you and you can see the underside of the toenail. The dog can receive a treat and a belly rub after each clip of a nail.

With the file or grinder or dremel tool, smooth down the rough nail. Train sensitive dogs not to fear the electric tool by introducing it to them a little at a time: At first, introduce the tool itself; next, the tool turned on but not touching the dog; and finally, tiny bits of touching the paw at a time. Reward your dog's brave investigation of the tool throughout the process with lots of praise and treats.

For extra polish and shine, rub a tiny bit of baby oil on each nail and on paw pads to keep them moist. Don't rub on too much, however, as it will make your dog's feet slippery. Or, instead of a drop of oil, give your pampered pooch a dash of color with nail polish made just for dogs.

And that's it. Your dog's nails are pretty, and pretty healthy, too. Clip them often, keeping them short, and you'll preserve your dog's feet, legs, and mobility while you help accustom your dog to the handling of his feet.

You're almost done with that monthly grooming routine, but first it's time to check just a few more parts to ensure that your dog is in good health and perfect hygiene.

Part 2

Eyes, Ears, Teeth, and Rears

Now that your dog is brushed, washed, dried, and has his toenails clipped, you just have a few more things to do to complete the monthly grooming routine: give your dog's eyes, ears, teeth, and rear the once-over.

These areas of your dog's body all require proper hygiene, maintenance, and attention. Neglected eyes, ears, teeth, and rears can all become unsightly and even infected, so do your dog a favor and keep these areas well maintained. You could save a lot of money on vet care, not to mention avoiding pain and suffering for your dog.

All areas of your dog's body require proper hygiene and maintenance.

Part 2

The right products can help you keep your dog's ears clean and healthy.

A toothbrush and toothpaste made for dogs are crucial parts of your grooming equipment.

You will need these tools and products for this portion of the monthly grooming session:

• Moisturizing eye drops (for dogs with dry eyes) or canine eyewash

• Tear-stain remover (for light-colored dogs, if tear stains are a problem)

• Ear hair tweezers and/or small scissors

• Ear powder

• Ear wash or mineral oil

• Toothbrush or a piece of gauze big enough to wrap around your finger

• Toothpaste made for dogs

• Small spray bottle

• Dental scaler, for heavy plaque deposits

• Heavy gauze for emptying anal glands, if necessary

• Cotton balls

• Cotton swabs.

The Eyes Have It

First, take a good look at your dog's eyes. Depending on the breed, the eyes may be receded, narrow, almond-shaped, almost round, or round and slightly protruding. Different eye types need different kinds of care.

• The protruding eyes of brachycephalic, or flat-faced, dogs require the most care because they are less protected than eyes that are set deeper and protected by a long muzzle. They dry out easily and are easily injured.

• Dogs with white fur may develop tear stains from the eyes.

• Dogs with entropion, a condition in which the lid turns inward and eyelashes irritate the cornea, need special attention and, in extreme cases, surgery to correct the problem.

• Dogs with excessive tearing need the eye area to be kept clean and dry.

• Dogs with dry eyes require moisturizing eye drops every day.

Check your dog's eyes every day, not just monthly. Most dogs occasionally accumulate debris in the corners of their eyes, and they will benefit from wiping the face down with a moist cloth and cleaning the corners of the eyes with a moist cotton ball every day (don't wipe the cotton ball over the eye or you could scratch the cornea).

Many dogs with protruding eyes require a daily dose of moisturizing eye drops to keep their eyes moist and comfortable. (Some brands of human eye drops work, but check with your vet about which brand to use.) If you check, clean, and moisturize your dog's eyes every day, he will soon get used to the ritual.

Dogs with protruding or very large eyes need special care and attention.

Light-coated dogs may develop tear stains under their eyes, which can be treated with daily cleaning and a tear-stain remover.

Part 2

Your veterinarian should examine your dog's eyes at his regular checkup.

Eye Alert

Always be careful of your dog's eyes during grooming, especially if your dog has protruding eyes. Scissors, clippers, even brushes and combs could seriously injure an eye if you aren't paying attention. Always have the points of scissors or the edges of clippers pointing away from the eyes. Try to use blunt-tipped scissors near the eyes and ears.

During monthly sessions, rinse your dog's eyes with the canine eyewash or eye drops. Put a drop in each eye and carefully wipe away the excess from the corners with a soft cloth or dry cotton ball.

If your light-coated dog has tear stains–brownish streaks under the eyes–be very diligent about wiping eyes clean daily, and apply a tear-stain remover to the stained fur (not to the eyes themselves) according to the directions for the individual product.

If your dog seems to be tearing excessively, so that even when you wipe his eyes clean every day he is still constantly wet under the eyes, or if you notice unusual redness or swollen areas in or around the eye, please consult your vet. Dogs can develop many different minor eye disorders that are easily treated. Also check that the eyes are clear. Cloudiness could mean your dog is developing cataracts.

Finally, a yearly vet exam is crucial to keeping eyes healthy, and your vet can help to detect eye diseases in the early stages so they can best be treated.

Ear Ye, Ear Ye

Whether your dog's ears are long and droopy or short and catlike, they require attention. Ears produce wax, trap dirt, grow hair, retain moisture, and can easily develop infections when they aren't kept clean, plucked, and dry.

Check your dog's ears every day. If your dog is used to ear handling, he will be more comfortable with it when a professional groomer or vet has to touch his ears. Then, during the monthly grooming session, spend a little more time on those ears.

1. First, examine your dog's ears. Check the outside for tangles and parasites, which often gravitate toward the ears. Check the insides for dirt and excessive wax buildup. Your dog's ears should be clean. A little ear wax is normal, but ask your vet about large amounts, or ear wax that looks reddish brown or streaky or smells funny.

2. Next, check for hair inside the ear. Ear hair can trap dirt, bacteria, and moisture inside the ear canal, causing infection. Trimming ear hair also makes the ears appear neater and more attractive.

3. To trim ear hair, first pull the ear back over the dog's head, laying it flat against the skull. This will shut off the delicate parts of the ear canal.

4. For long ear hair, pluck out individual hairs with your fingers. If you find this difficult, dip your fingers in a little ear powder to make it easier to grasp ear hairs. Don't pluck out more than two hairs at one time, as this could be painful to your dog. Use ear hair forceps–small tweezers made for plucking ear hair. Again, only pluck one or two hairs at a time.

Dogs with long ears can get dirt trapped beneath the ear flap and require special care.

Use small, blunt-tipped scissors to clip ear hair.

Keeping your dog's ears clean will reduce the chance of ear infection.

Dogs need assistance in keeping their teeth clean and free of plaque.

5. For shorter hair that is hard to pluck, or if you prefer to cut rather than pluck, clip ear hair with a small, blunt-tipped scissors.

6. Dust ears with medicated ear powder if they are prone to infection.

7. If ears are very dirty, gently pull the ear out away from the skull to open up the ear canal and place a few drops of ear wash or mineral oil in the ear. Massage the base of the ear to work the cleanser down the canal. Hold the ear down for a minute to let the fluid enter the ear canal, then release your dog and let him shake his head a few times to loosen ear wax. Check ears again and clean out loosened wax with a cotton ball or cotton swab dipped in ear wash or mineral oil.

8. For drop-eared dogs, keep all hair under the ear opening and on the inside flap of the ear trimmed short. This will increase air flow to the ear and reduce the likelihood of ear infections.

Pearly Whites

Dog teeth may be longer and sharper than human teeth, but they develop plaque and tartar in the same way we do. When the clear, sticky plaque film isn't brushed away, it hardens and develops into ugly brown tartar that can compromise gum integrity and result in infection. Oral infections are particularly dangerous because they can quickly travel to the heart, and more than a few dogs have become extremely ill (or worse) due to neglected dental care.

You can tell when your dog has tartar buildup: Tartar is the hard brown stuff that sticks to your dog's teeth,

Treats and Toys for Better Teeth

Dogs that eat hard, crunchy dog biscuits and hard kibble enjoy the benefits of natural teeth cleaning from these treats. (Choose treats made with natural ingredients and low in preservatives if you can.) Avoid feeding soft, unhealthy "people food." Many dog toys, such as Nylabones®, are also designed specifically to clean teeth, so let your dog enjoy these chew toys as well. But don't let biscuits and toys do the whole job. For ideal dental care, you should still brush and check your dog's teeth at least once a week.

Safe chew toys can keep your dog's teeth clean and healthy.

Part 2

and you can't just brush it away. It must be scraped with a dental scaler. Some people like to try this themselves; others leave the job to their vets. But you can prevent tartar buildup by keeping your dog's teeth cleaned of plaque. Don't wait until the monthly grooming session to brush your dog's teeth. Do it once a week, or even better, once a day as part of the daily grooming session. Keep those pearly whites…well, pearly white!

Some dogs don't mind having their teeth brushed, but others rebel against the process and need to be introduced to the tools and methods of dental care gradually and with lots of rewards.

First, let your dog sniff the toothbrush and lick some of the toothpaste off your finger. Praise your dog for investigating.

The next day, let your dog sniff the toothbrush again, and touch it against your dog's muzzle. Again, praise and reward your dog with a treat.

If your dog doesn't like the taste of doggy toothpaste, don't worry—the point isn't to eat it. The point is to get your dog used to the taste of the toothpaste and to the feel of the brush.

Let your dog become accustomed to the toothbrush slowly; eventually he will come to accept it.

The next day, speaking calmly and reassuringly to your dog, take his muzzle in your hand and part his lips along the side. Touch the brush to his teeth, then immediately praise and reward him.

On the following day, rub the brush against his teeth for just a few seconds. Praise and reward. If at any point during this process your dog gets nervous or scared, back up a step, but don't give up.

Finally, put a little toothpaste (or a baking soda and water paste) on the toothbrush and rub it briefly on your dog's teeth.

Brush your dog's teeth for a slightly longer period each time you try it, until your dog is so used to the process that he enjoys the attention. (Don't forget the lavish praise!)

Once your dog is used to having his teeth brushed, the following procedure will ensure you do a good and thorough job. Here's how to brush your dog's teeth, step by step.

• Using a soft toothbrush or one designed for dogs, put a small amount of toothpaste on the brush, or put toothpaste on a piece of gauze wrapped around your finger.

• Open your dog's mouth, exposing his teeth, and brush both teeth and gums as you would brush your own teeth.

• Make sure you brush along the gum line, where plaque and tartar accumulate first.

• Don't press too hard, or you could injure your dog's gums.

Use a soft toothbrush or one that is specially designed for dogs.

Toothy Tools

You can buy all kinds of toothbrush-inspired products designed to clean your dog's teeth. All you really need is a regular soft toothbrush and toothpaste made for dogs (human toothpaste has ingredients that aren't healthy for your dog). However, you can also buy bristled rubber fingertip toothbrushes that fit over your index finger, different sizes and shapes of toothbrushes, tooth-brushing sponges, dental spray (like mouthwash for dogs), toys like the Chew-n-Brush, and even breath freshener.

If your dog has excessive tartar, you may want to use a dental scraper to clean his teeth.

• Avoid any red, irritated, or infected-looking areas, and tell your vet about them.

• If your dog has excessive tartar (most common on top teeth), use the dental scraper to carefully scrape teeth from just under the gum line to the tip. Protect gums with your fingers and be careful not to scrape your dog's gums, or make a vet appointment to have this done professionally, especially if tartar deposits are very heavy.

• Spray your dog's mouth with water to rinse off the toothpaste and debris, and you're done!

On a monthly basis, do more than a cursory oral check. Look carefully for changes, tartar accumulation, loose teeth, and red areas that could signal a gum infection. Let your vet know about any suspicious-looking changes. Remember, dental infections can travel straight to your dog's heart, so don't ignore them!

A NYlabone® can help keep your dog's mouth healthy.

The Notorious Anal Glands

All dogs have anal glands located on either side of the rectum. These glands produce a pungent brown fluid and should empty naturally when your dog defecates. However, in many dogs, these glands become blocked or even impacted and must be emptied by hand. It's not a pretty job, but somebody has to do it! Your dog may never need his anal glands emptied, but if yours does, you can pay your vet a lot of money to do it, you can beg and plead and bribe a professional groomer to do it, or you can do it yourself.

Dogs who are accustomed to lots of grooming-related handling may not mind this process, and dogs who are used to it don't mind it at all. In fact, it probably relieves some discomfort. Signs your dog's anal glands need to be emptied include scooting along the floor or excessive licking to the area.

Your dog's anal glands can become impacted and may need to be emptied, either by a groomer or a vet.

The anal glands are located below the rectum at four o'clock and eight o'clock. To empty them, first place a square of gauze over the rectum to catch the fluid, which will spurt or ooze out. Using your thumb and index finger, push out, down, and inward to empty the glands. You may need to try it a few times, but don't do so to the point of upsetting your dog. If you can't seem to do it, have your vet or groomer show you how. (It's worth paying for an office visit to get this instruction.)

If you empty the anal glands during the bath, it will be easy to rinse the fluid away. If you do so afterward or on a day when you aren't giving your dog a bath, catch the fluid with the gauze pad or expel the glands outside, then clean the area with a warm washcloth.

Just the Beginning

Now that we've covered the basics of the monthly grooming session, it's time to take a closer look at what kind of coat care your individual breed requires. In the next section, we'll show you how to care for, cut, clip, and otherwise beautify your dog's individual coat type.

Part Three

Coat-Specific Grooming Guide

HAIRY

POOFY

FUZZY

'BIKER'

Know your dog's coat type.

Grooming the Smooth and Medium Coat

The smooth and medium coats are by far the easiest to groom. People who show dogs with smooth and medium coats in dog shows often admit they chose the dogs they now obsess about because they can "wash and go" from bathtub to show ring with virtually no effort at all. Many of these breeds are shown in a completely natural state. Others require only very small amounts of trimming here and there to neaten areas of longer or shaggier hair growth. In general, however, smooth and medium coats are the lazy groomer's dream.

However easy to groom the shorter coats may be, you can do many things to make them look great. In this chapter, we will first discuss smooth coats,

Smooth and medium-coated dogs are the easiest to groom.

It doesn't take much work to get your smooth-coated dog ready for the show ring.

What About Your Breed?

In most cases, grooming smooth coats or medium coats will be about the same for all the breeds with these coat types. However, a few individuals have certain coat specifications related to dog showing. Because this is a book primarily for at-home pet groomers, we won't always go into breed specifics. Pet grooming on many breeds is virtually identical. For more on how to groom all the individual breeds for the show ring, check out a breed-specific grooming book. A list of these can be found in the Resources section in the back of this book or check the breed club website for specific information.

and then medium coats, giving you some helpful hints and tricks for keeping these coats looking their best.

Grooming the Smooth Coat

First let's look at the smooth coat. Sleek, hard, glossy, and shape-defining, the smooth coat is probably the easiest of all coat types to groom because beyond brushing and the occasional bath, they don't require anything at all–no clipping, no shaving, no trimming, no shaping, not even a blow-dry! Some dogs have their whiskers trimmed or certain areas neatened with a clipper for the show ring, but these details aren't necessary for pets.

The two best things you can do to keep the smooth coat shiny and healthy are to brush often and bathe seldom.

Part 3

Easy On Bath Time

Smooth-coated breeds tend to have sensitive skin (there are exceptions). Too-frequent bathing can deplete the natural oils that give smooth coats their characteristic sheen, so don't worry about bathing your smooth-coated dog more than a couple of times a year, unless he gets really dirty, such as after a swim in a lake, a day hunting out in the field, or if he rolls in, gets into, or tangles with something smelly (a dead animal, garbage, or a skunk).

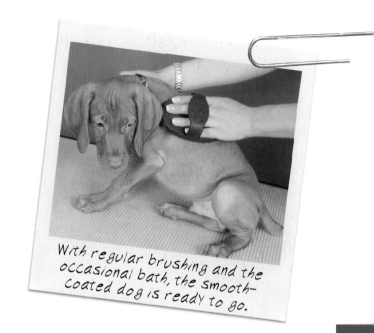

With regular brushing and the occasional bath, the smooth-coated dog is ready to go.

Though you don't *need* to brush your smooth-coated dog every day, you certainly *can*. Your dog will enjoy the feeling and the time spent with you. He will get used to brushing quickly. Plus you'll keep the skin stimulated, the oil distributed over the coat, and the coat free of shed hairs, dirt, and even parasites. In fact, daily brushing could keep some dogs completely flea-free without the use of chemicals all year long (depending on where you live, the flea population in your area, and how often your dog goes outside–see later chapters for more on parasite prevention and treatment).

As a review, here are the smooth-coated breeds. If your breed is in this list, or if your mixed-breed dog has a smooth coat, use the instructions in this section.

The Boxer's sleek coat is representative of a smooth-coated breed.

Smooth-Coated Breeds

American Foxhound	Chinese Crested (hairless)	Labrador Retriever
American Staffordshire Terrier	Dalmatian	Manchester Terrier (Toy and Standard)
Anatolian Shepherd	Dachshund (smooth)	
Basenji	Doberman Pinscher	Mastiff
Basset Hound	English Foxhound	Miniature Pinscher
Beagle	Fox Terrier (smooth)	Pointer
Black and Tan Coonhound	French Bulldog	Pharoah Hound
Bloodhound	German Shorthaired Pointer	Pug
Boston Terrier	Great Dane	Rhodesian Ridgeback
Boxer	Greater Swiss Mountain Dog	Rottweiler
Bulldog	Greyhound	Staffordshire Bull Terrier
Bullmastiff	Harrier	Toy Fox Terrier
Bull Terrier	Ibizan Hound	Vizsla
Chihuahua (smooth)	Italian Greyhound	Weimeraner
Chinese Sharpei	Jack Russell Terrier (Smooth)	Whippet

Smooth-coated breeds can have sensitive skin, so be careful not to overbathe them.

The following are the core tools for grooming the smooth coat.

- Natural bristle brush

- Hound glove

- Rubber curry brush

- Chamois, flannel, silk, or velvet squares for polishing

- Coat conditioner spray or baby oil.

Once a day–or at least once a week–give your smooth-coated dog a good brushing.

1. Begin with a thorough rub-down with the hound glove.

2. Remove dead hair and dirt with the rubber curry brush.

3. Brush the coat smooth with the natural bristle brush.

4. Polish the coat with the fabric square.

5. For special occasions (or just to make your dog look extra shiny), lightly spray the coat with coat conditioner or put a few drops of baby oil in your palms, rub them together, and smooth over your dog's coat.

Instant beauty!

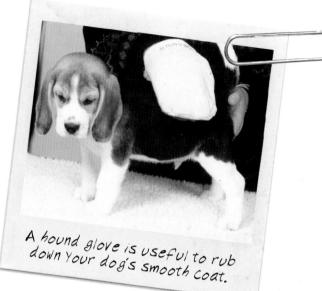

A hound glove is useful to rub down your dog's smooth coat.

Grooming the Medium Coat

Also easy to groom, many medium-coated dogs should remain completely natural without trimming, clipping, or shaping. The medium coat doesn't mat, tangle, hold on to dirt, or require much attention at all beyond regular brushing and the occasional bath.

As a general guideline, you can make slight adjustments to improve the shape of your dog by trimming head vs. body to balance an uneven dog, and attending to certain areas–such as clipping neck, neatening ears, and cleaning face with an electric clipper–in accordance with established show grooming for your breed. Spaniels and retrievers need hair removed from beneath the ears to improve airflow, and any long hair on the feet should be trimmed, especially between toe pads where mats form.

The medium-coated dog should always look completely natural without trimming or shaping.

Your Pseudo-Show Dog

A few medium-coated breeds do require special trimming or neatening for the show ring, and as a pet owner, you may enjoy making certain alterations to your pet's medium coat. Talk to your groomer or breeder, or consult a book that goes in-depth into breed-specific grooming. Even if your dog isn't a show dog, he can be as well groomed as one.

The sporting spaniels have the top third of their ears trimmed with clippers or thinning shears. The ruff on a spaniel's neck can be trimmed to an inch above the breastbone and blended into the shoulders. The other breeds with medium coats require very little trimming.

When relevant, you can also make small adjustments in shaping the ruff, rear furnishings, and ear hair, but in general, leave your medium-coated breed in a natural state, only neatening stray hairs without actually changing the dog's outline. The basic rule for medium-coated dogs is to brush often to remove shed hair. Less grooming is more.

As a reminder, below are the medium-coated breeds. If your breed is among them, or if your mixed-breed dog has a medium coat, follow the instructions in this section.

Medium-Coated Breeds

Akita	Cardigan Welsh Corgi	Kuvasz
Alaskan Malamute	Cavalier King Charles Spaniel	Norwegian Elkhound
American Eskimo Dog	Chesapeake Bay Retriever	Pembroke Welsh Corgi
Australian Cattle Dog	Clumber Spaniel	Saint Bernard
Australian Shepherd	Collie (smooth)	Saluki
Belgian Malinois	Dandie Dinmont Terrier	Schipperke
Belgian Sheepdog	English Springer Spaniel	Siberian Husky
Belgian Tervuren	Field Spaniel	Shiba Inu
Bernese Mountain Dog	Finnish Spitz	Spinone Italiano
Borzoi	Flat-Coated Retriever	Sussex Spaniel
Border Collie	German Shepherd Dog	Tibetan Spaniel
Brittany	Golden Retriever	Welsh Springer Spaniel
Canaan Dog	Great Pyrenees	

The core tools for grooming the medium coat are as follows:

• Pin brush

• Coat rake

• Hound glove

• Shedding comb

• Rubber curry brush

• Blow-dryer with low or cool setting.

Treats can keep your dog occupied while you are grooming him.

Every day, or at least once a week, give your dog a good brushing (as described in the chapter on brushing). During your monthly grooming sessions, after your dog has been bathed, follow this procedure.

1. Dry the medium coat with a towel. Air-drying the rest of the way is fine for medium-coats if you don't mind waiting a little longer for the coat to dry, especially in the case of thick double coats. Or, finish with a blow-dryer.

2. To blow-dry, set the blow-dryer on low or cool and blow-dry the coat as you brush with a pin brush or natural bristle brush in the direction of hair growth. If the brush pulls out more dead coat, even better.

3. Once your dog is completely dry, have him stand. Step back and take a good look at his outline. Compare it to a picture of a well-groomed show dog of the same

If you plan on showing your dog, you must groom him to conform to the breed standard.

A coat conditioner can keep your dog's coat easy to brush and looking radiant.

Give your medium-coated dog a good brushing at least a few times a week.

breed. How is the outline of the coat like or unlike the picture? Look for long, stray hairs, too-shaggy areas, or other imbalances.

4. Using a clipper, scissors, or a stripping knife (for plucking hairs, although you can do this with your fingers), neaten your dog's outline. Clip off hairs longer than the ones around them and straighten shaggy outlines that aren't supposed to be shaggy.

5. Never clip more than a few hairs without stopping and standing back to look again. If you trim at close range for too long, you can easily overdo the job. Remember, for medium coats, less is more!

6. Finally, and optionally, spray your dog's coat with a little coat conditioner to keep it resilient and easy to brush.

And that's all there is to grooming the medium coat. Aren't you glad you chose such an easy-care breed?

Grooming the Long Coat

Nothing quite compares to the glory of a perfectly groomed, long-coated dog trotting around the show ring, silky tresses flowing. It's no wonder the long-coated breeds so often win Best in Show! When it comes to grooming, the long coat is a true challenge, but one many pet owners relish.

In this chapter, long-coated breeds are divided into three categories: those whose hair is parted down the middle and groomed accordingly; small long-coated dogs; and large long-coated dogs. Within each of these categories are different breeds, but grooming within each category is similar. Instructions are for all dogs within a category, with particular notes on individual

Grooming the long coat is a challenge, but the results are worth it.

Part 3

The Shih Tzu is just one of the long-haired breeds whose coat is parted along the back.

The Growing Afghan

Afghan puppies should be groomed with a parted coat. However, once Afghans reach maturity, they grow in a smooth, short-haired saddle along the back so that they no longer require parting. For this reason, the Afghan *puppy* is a parted-coat breed. The mature Afghan is actually a long-coated large breed and should be groomed accordingly. The biggest grooming challenge of the Afghan at any age? Time! It takes a long time to keep the tangles out of so much coat.

breeds with a unique grooming requirement (such as the double topknot on the Maltese).

As with previous chapters, this is not a guide to high-end dog show grooming. This is a general guide for the pet owner who would like to keep the long-coated dog in its full coat. For more detailed show grooming instructions on your particular breed of long-coated dog, visit a professional groomer or breeder or contact your breed's national club for grooming information.

Long Hair, Parted Coat

There are eight breeds that have very long hair that should be parted along the back. Although other breeds have long hair, and some breeds (such as the Bearded Collie) may have hair that falls into a natural part, these eight breeds should be groomed with a very deliberate, perfectly straight part from the nape of the neck to the base of the tail.

Parted Coats

The following are breeds with parted coats.

Afghan Hound	Shih Tzu
Lhasa Apso	Silky Terrier
Maltese	Tibetan Terrier
Skye Terrier	Yorkshire Terrier

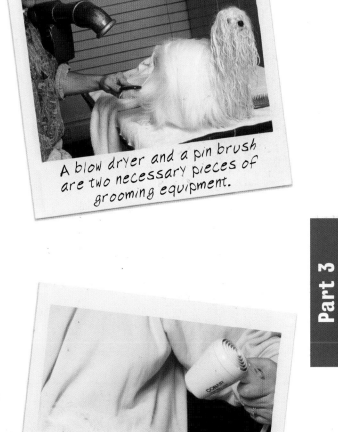

A blow dryer and a pin brush are two necessary pieces of grooming equipment.

You will need the following tools to groom your parted-coat breed:

• Pin brush

• Slicker brush (for daily mat removal in pets)

• Comb (fine, medium, or wide, depending on coat thickness)

• Scissors, for shaping and trimming (when relevant)

• Electric clippers with a #10 blade (except for Afghans) plus a #15 blade for Yorkshire Terriers

• Blow-dryer with cool setting

• Protein coat conditioner

Start by blow drying sections of your dog's coat, moving from the bottom up to the top of the dog.

Part 3

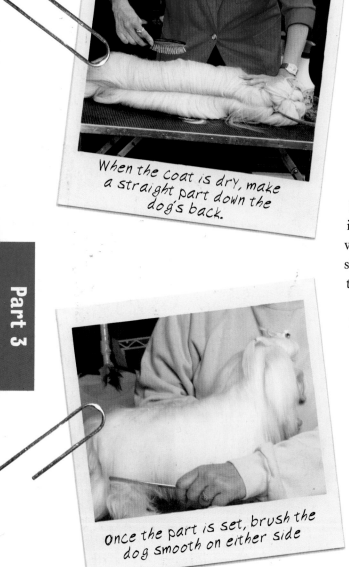

When the coat is dry, make a straight part down the dog's back.

Once the part is set, brush the dog smooth on either side

• Rubber bands, bows, ribbons, barrettes, etc., if you want to tie up your dog's topknot.

Parted-Coat Grooming, Step by Step

Parting these coats is arguably the most difficult part of grooming them, aside from a simple time investment to keep the coats mat-free. Here is your step-by-step, post-bath method for grooming your long, parted-coat breed.

1. After towel-drying, blow-dry the long coat to keep it from drying into tangles. With the blow-dryer on cool or low, work from the bottom up, taking sections of hair with the pin brush and holding them out from the body. Keep the blow-dryer moving over each piece of hair until it is dry, then move up. Start with the legs and rear end and work your way up and forward. Keep brushing, fluffing, and straightening the coat so it dries smoothly and free from tangles.

2. When the coat is dry, or almost dry, make the part. Stand behind your dog and put the tip of the comb just over the nose, then slowly, an inch or two at a time, move the comb over the crown of the head, down the nape, and down the back to the base of the tail. As you go, carefully move the hairs to the proper side.

3. If you finish and the part looks crooked, try again. It's good practice. Making a perfectly straight part isn't easy, but once you know how to do it, you'll feel like a pro. Be patient.

4. Once the coat is parted, spray it with coat conditioner or coat dressing to set the part. Now you can work on brushing the dog smooth on either side of the part.

5. Just as before the bath, brush thoroughly, using the pin brush (or the slicker brush for heavily coated pets who still need some tangles removed) starting from the bottom and the back of the dog and working your way up and forward. Make sure the hair lies smoothly and is tangle-free on either side of the part.

6. With a #10 blade on your electric clipper, shave your dog's anal area to keep it clean and free of long hair and tangles. Be careful not to touch the blade directly on your dog's skin. Or, clip the area neatly with a scissors.

7. With the same #10 blade, shave your dog's abdomen from groin to naval and down the insides of both thighs, except for Afghans, which should not be shaved.

8. Trim between your dog's paw pads with a scissors, and trim around his feet so the hair just reaches the ground evenly around the paw in a rounded shape.

9. If your dog's coat reaches the ground, scissor it neatly at floor level to keep it from interfering with your pet's movement.

10. Brush out the hair on your dog's head, ears, and face.

11. If desired, tie up the topknot.

Tying the Topknot

The topknot is an attractive way to keep long hair out of your dog's eyes. The tied-up, ribbon-bedecked topknot is a traditional grooming practice for the Maltese, Shih Tzu, and Yorkshire Terrier, and

Shave your dog's abdomen from groin to navel and down the inside of both thighs.

Yorkie Ears

With most small breeds, the ears are left naturally, except for plucking of stray hairs inside the ears. Yorkshire Terriers, however, should have neater, catlike ears kept free of fringe. Shave the tips of your Yorkie's ears with a #15 blade, inside and out, to a half-inch, and scissor the hair to neaten.

Part 3

The topknot is an attractive way to keep your dog's hair out of his eyes.

sometimes for the Afghan and the Lhasa Apso. The Skye Terrier, Tibetan Terrier, and Silky Terrier don't traditionally wear a topknot (Silky Terriers can usually see fine without one), but just because your breed isn't formally groomed with a topknot doesn't mean you can't tie one on anyway. Your long-haired pet may enjoy actually being able to *see* you!

To tie a topknot on your part-coated dog:

• Part your dog's hair over each ear, and in a line from ear-to-ear behind the ears. Draw the topknot together in your hands.

• Secure with a latex rubber band (you can buy these from a groomer). Be careful not to attach the rubber band so that it pulls the hairs too tightly. A topknot should be a relief, not a pain.

• If desired, attach a bow or a barrette. You can buy an amazing array of hair accessories at pet stores and on the Internet. Or, braid the topknot and attach a latex rubberband at the end of the braid.

The Maltese traditionally wears two topknots, one on each side of his head.

The Maltese Headpiece

Most long-haired small breeds with a tied-up topknot wear a single tie in the center of the head. The Maltese, however, traditionally wears its topknot tied on either side of the part. To tie up the Maltese top-knots, use the original middle part as a guide. Then, part over each ear and make two topknots, one on either side of the part. Attach a latex rubber band and ribbon or barrette to each.

Grooming the Long-Haired Small Breeds

Next, let's turn to the long-haired small breeds whose coats aren't parted along the back. These frisky little long-haired fellows need lots of attention to their coats. Although none of these breeds have the sheer length of the part-coated breeds, they all have long coats that can mat, tangle, and compromise both their beauty and good health.

The small breeds are easy to groom on a grooming table or even a bathroom counter. They tend to thrive on the attention and pampering of regular grooming sessions, and they love to spend that time with their people. Because many of these breeds live inside the house, they don't tend to get into underbrush or dirt as often (although a good romp in a muddy yard or dog park can result in an extended grooming session). However, these coats still need attention and plenty of it.

Some of the breeds listed need more frequent brushing and combing than others because some have longer and/or thicker hair than others. However, a daily grooming session is perfect for any small, long-coated breed, whether they really need it or not. They *think* they need it, and they are quite certain they *deserve* it. (And who could argue?)

You will need these tools to groom your long-coated small dog.

• Pin brush

• Slicker brush (for daily mat removal in pets)

Long-haired small breeds, like the Papillon, need lots of attention to their coats.

The longhaired Dachshund needs more coat care than his short-haired brothers.

Long-Coated Small Breeds

The long-coated small breeds are:

Chihuahua (longhaired)

Chinese Crested (powderpuff)

Longhaired Dachshund

English Toy Spaniel

Havanese

Japanese Chin

Löwchen

Papillion

Pekingese

Pomeranian

- Comb (fine, medium, or wide, depending on coat thickness)

- Scissors, for shaping and trimming (when relevant)

- Electric clippers with a #10 blade

- Blow-dryer with cool setting

- Protein coat conditioner.

Havanese: No Bow Zone

Most of the long-coated small breeds without parted coats don't wear tied-up topknots, but because the Havanese has a long fall of hair, its topknot can be tied with an elastic band or braided or secured with barrettes on either side of the part. Although in its native Cuba the Havanese fall of hair protects this little breed's eyes from the sun and the topknot is never tied up, pet owners in this country often keep the hair out of their pets' eyes. However, according to the Havanese breed standard, groomers should never put bows or ribbons on the Havanese topknot. (If you would like to put one on your pet, we promise not to tell!)

Long-Coated Small Dog Grooming, Step by Step

The long-coated small breeds are characterized by a certain charming full fluffiness, as opposed to the parted-coat breeds, which are characterized by long, smooth, flowing hair, more akin to long human hair. For this reason, groom these dogs with fullness in mind: Think of the coat standing out from the body, rather than lying flat against the skin.

Part 3

After you've bathed your little dog, here is how to groom that long fluffy coat, step by step.

1. After towel-drying, blow-dry the long coat to keep it from drying into tangles. With the blow-dryer on cool or low, work from the bottom up, using the pin brush or slicker brush to fluff-dry. Take sections of hair with the pin brush or slicker brush and hold them out from the body as you blow-dry.

2. Keep the blow-dryer moving over each piece of hair until it is dry, then move up. Start with the legs and rear end and work your way up and forward. Keep brushing and fluffing for fullness, keeping the coat free from tangles.

3. Finish by running a metal comb through the coat to ensure that you haven't missed a single tangle or snag.

4. With a #10 blade on your electric clipper, shave your dog's anal area to keep it clean and free of long hair and tangles. Be careful not to touch the blade directly on your dog's skin. Or, if you prefer, clip the area neatly with scissors.

5. Optionally, depending on your breed or if you like the ease of having your dog's underside free of long hair, with the same #10 blade, shave your dog's abdomen from groin to naval and down the insides of both thighs. Shave *with* the lay of the hair.

6. Trim between your dog's paw pads with scissors, and if hair covers the feet, trim around the feet so the hair just reaches the ground evenly around the paw in a rounded shape.

Some of the smaller breeds are characterized by the fullness and fluffiness of their coats.

Run a comb through your dog's hair to ensure you haven't missed any tangles or snags.

To finish grooming the dog, fluff any area that has a profuse coat, like his tail, ruff, or chest.

The Havanese looks like a parted-coat breed, but his coat should be left natural.

7. Brush and comb the hair on your dog's head, ears, and face.

8. Stand back and look at the dog's shape. Scissor any stray long hairs but don't actually change the shape of the coat. Just look for uneven, stray areas that stand out after brushing.

9. To finish the dog and take most advantage of fluffiness, spray the coat with coat conditioner or coat dressing to keep it soft and in place, then brush lightly over the top of the coat to set. Brush from bottom up and from shoulders forward to fluff the ruff. Fluff the tail, the body, the chest, the fringe—any area in which your long-haired small dog has a profuse coat.

10. Admire the beauty!

Breed-Specific Notes

A few of the breeds in this category have special grooming requirements.

Havanese

The Havenese looks like a parted-coat breed, but its silky coat shouldn't be artificially parted. It may fall into a part, however, and this is natural. Some Havanese also have very wavy coats, which can naturally fall into cords. This is an acceptable coat type for the Havanese, making it look more like one of the curly-coated, corded breeds (which include the Puli and the Komondor). If desired, tie up the Havenese topknot into a braid or elastic band.

Löwchen

The French Löwchen is often clipped to look like a

Long Coats, Dry Coats

Long coats easily become dry and brittle, and they should never be brushed dry. For daily brushing as well as postbath brushing, always spray long coats with a moisturizing coat conditioner and finish with a light spray of coat gloss containing oil. Regular moisturizing of long coats will keep them from breaking and splitting, resulting in a softer, fluffier, healthier, and more attractive coat.

lion, with the hindquarters and base of the tail completely shaved, the head and ruff left full like a mane, and the tuft of the tail left full so it can swish like a lion's tail. However, some people choose not to shave their little Löwchens in this way, preferring to leave the coat long or cut them down into a puppy cut for ease of care.

If you choose to groom your Löwchen according to the breed standard, use a one eighth-inch comb on your electric clipper. Shave from the last rib back, leaving the full coat on the dog so that it covers the last rib. Shave the hindquarters all the way down to the hock or heel joint (remember, in dogs the heel is the first joint up above the ground, not down by the paw), leaving a cuff of hair around the base of the foot. Clip the front legs from the elbow to the dewclaws (or to where they used to be if they are removed) so that the cuff of coat on the front legs matches the back legs in height. Clip the tail from the base to about halfway down the coat, leaving a tail plume. As for the rest of your Lowchen, the breed standard states that all unclipped areas should be left completely natural without any trimming, shaping, or scissoring. Do keep that Löwchen brushed and combed, however; otherwise, you'll have an unhappily matted little dog.

Chinese Crested

The Chinese Crested comes in two varieties: hairless and powderpuff. To groom your hairless Chinese Crested, lightly brush the long tufts of hair on the head, ears, face, tail, and feet. To keep the hairless skin in good condition, moisturize

The Chinese Crested comes in two varieties: the Hairless and the Powderpuff.

Part 3

your dog's skin by rubbing a few drops of baby oil between your palms and massaging it over the dog's body. For the powderpuff variety, groom your Chinese Crested according to the previous instructions to keep the long coat tangle-free and fluffy.

Pekingese and Pomeranian

Once they are dry, brush the Pekingese and the Pomeranian against the lay of the hair to most dramatically enhance the powder puff effect of the coat.

That Wrinkly Peke

The Pekingese has distinctive facial wrinkles, so be sure to keep these clean and dry.

Grooming the Long-Haired Large Breeds

The long-haired large breeds are groomed similarly to the small breeds, but these larger, long-coated dogs have some unique challenges of their own. The long-coated large breeds are more likely than their smaller counterparts to be working dogs, and spending time out in the field, the tundra, or the woods can result in a tangled, dirty, or debris-filled coat. Regular grooming and thorough brushing and combing is essential to keep the working dog's long coat healthy.

You will need these tools to groom your long-coated large breed.

- Large pin brush

- Large slicker brush (for daily mat removal in pets)

- Steel comb (medium or wide, depending on coat thickness)

- Coat rake

- Natural bristle brush

- Scissors, for shaping and trimming (when relevant)

Regular grooming and brushing are essential to keep the coat of the larger breeds healthy.

Part 3

Long-Haired Large Breeds

The long-coated large breeds include the following:

Bearded Collie

Briard

Chow Chow

Cocker Spaniel

Collie (rough)

English Cocker Spaniel

English Setter

Gordon Setter

Irish Setter

Keeshond

Newfoundland

Old English Sheepdog

Polish Lowland Sheepdog

Saint Bernard (longhaired)

Samoyed

Shetland Sheepdog

The long-haired large breeds take a long time to groom, due to the abundant amount of hair.

• Electric clippers with a #10 blade

• Protein coat conditioner

• Blow-dryer with cool setting.

The long-coated large breeds have profuse hair that needs special care. They take a long time to groom because their size means they have so *much* of that thick, long coat.

Never brush a long-coated large dog without first spraying the coat with coat conditioner, or you could seriously compromise coat quality by breaking too much hair. Long coats dry out easily and can become brittle and fragile without conditioning. Before a bath, spray the dog well and brush out with a pin brush, working out tangled areas with the slicker brush and comb.

Part 3

Use a coat conditioner before brushing in order to limit the number of broken hairs.

Those Busy Breeds

Long-coated large breeds have some very important jobs.

- Gun dogs who help their humans hunt
- Highly athletic field trial competitors
- Herders on a sheep farm
- Cattle dogs out on the range
- Sled dogs, pulling sleds through the tundra
- Active family pets who accompany their people on hikes, runs, and camping expeditions.

This category includes many different breeds with various types of coats, but, in general, grooming instructions are the same. However, look for special instructions regarding the sporting breeds in this category, at the end of this section.

After the bath, here is how to groom your long-coated large dog.

1. After towel-drying thoroughly, blow-dry the long coat to keep it from drying into tangles. With the blow-dryer on cool or low, work from the bottom up, using the pin brush or slicker brush.

2. When the coat is dry, work through the coat from the skin out with a metal comb to ensure you haven't missed a single tangle or snag. If your dog is "blowing coat" or shedding, pull out excess coat with a coat rake. In heavily layered coats, work a layer at a time to be sure you aren't leaving tangles and mats close to the skin.

3. Shave your dog's anal area to keep it clean and free of long hair and tangles. Be careful not to touch the blade directly on your dog's skin. Or, clip the area neatly with a scissors.

4. Trim between your dog's paw pads with a scissors, and if hair covers the feet, trim around the feet so the hair just reaches the ground evenly around the paw in a rounded shape.

5. Brush and comb the hair on your dog's head, ears, and face. Pluck hair out of the ears to neaten.

6. Stand back and look at the dog's shape. Scissor any stray long hairs but don't actually change the shape of the coat. Just look for uneven, stray areas that stand out after brushing.

7. To finish the dog and keep the coat in good shape, spray once more with coat conditioner, then brush lightly over the top of the coat to set. Fluff the tail (when relevant for your breed), the ruff, the chest, the fringe–any area in which your long-haired large dog has profuse coat.

8. Give your very patient long-coated dog a nice treat. It took a long time to groom that coat!

The Long-Coated Sporting Breeds

Most of the long-coated large breeds must be carefully brushed and combed, but have natural coats that should not be shaped or clipped. The

Blow dry the coat to keep it from drying in tangles, working from the bottom to the top of the dog.

Tap the Pros

If you aren't confident shaving your long-haired sporting dog, have a professional groomer do it, or ask a groomer or the breeder to show you how. However, once you get used to the procedure, it's easy to clip your long-coated sporting breed in the correct way.

Brush and comb the hair on your dog's face, ears, and head.

Part 3

Scissor any stray hairs to neaten the shape of the coat.

sporting breeds are different. If you've chosen a long-coated sporting breed, grooming should include some very specific shaping with the electric clipper.

Special Instructions

Just follow these special instructions to groom your Cocker Spaniel, English Cocker Spaniel, English Setter, Gordon Setter, or Irish Setter after bathing and brushing. (See opposite page for individual clipping patterns.)

1. Clip the face along jawbone and cheeks and the top and back of the head to keep the face clean.

2. Clip under the jaw and down the neck to about one or two inches above the breastbone, blending into the chest area.

3. Clip hair about a third of the way down each ear. Use a #10 blade on your electric clipper for large areas, a #15 for smaller areas.

4. Clip the body, including the tail, with a #7 blade, in the direction of hair growth. Leave the coat long along the legs and chest. Gradually blend the shorter back hair into the longer hair to avoid an obvious clipper line.

5. Proceed according to the remaining steps for all long-coated breeds, above.

Part 3

English Setter

Cocker Spaniel

Irish Setter

Gordon Setter

Part 3

Grooming the Wire Coat

The wire coat is unique in texture and appearance: It gives that scruffy, whiskery character to the breeds that have it. The proper wire coat shouldn't be soft, fuzzy, or silky. It should be hard and crisp, like beard hair. It should also be groomed in a manner different than any other coat type, in order to maintain its crisp texture and to keep it bright in color and free of dead hairs.

Some pet owners choose to shave down their wirehaired pets rather than endure the task of properly grooming the wire coat. This is certainly an option for pet owners who don't mind a softer coat, but shaving the coat will cause it to grow back softer and silkier, and less characteristically wiry.

The wire coat is unique in both texture and appearance.

Wirehaired Breeds

The wirehaired breeds (sometimes called broken coated) are mostly terriers, with a few exceptions. They include the following:

Affenpinscher	German Wirehaired Pointer	Otterhound
Airedale Terrier	Schnauzer (Giant, Standard, and Miniature)	Petit Basset Griffon Vendeen
Australian Terrier		Scottish Deerhound
Border Terrier	Irish Terrier	Scottish Terrier
Bouvier des Flandres	Irish Wolfhound	Sealyham Terrier
Brussels Griffon	Parson (Jack) Russell Terrier (wirehaired)	Soft Coated Wheaten Terrier
Cairn Terrier		Welsh Terrier
Dachshund (wirehaired)	Lakeland Terrier	West Highland White Terrier
Dandie Dinmont Terrier	Norfolk Terrier	Wirehaired Pointing Griffon
Fox Terrier (wire)	Norwich Terrier	

Most of the wirehaired breeds are terriers, like the Scottish Terrier.

These tools are required to groom the wire coat.

- Natural bristle brush

- Slicker brush

- Hound glove or terrier mitt

- Combination medium/fine-toothed comb

- Shedding comb

- Stripping knife

- Scissors, for shaping and trimming

- Electric clippers with a variety of blade sizes as relevant for breed, for shaping and keeping anal area clean

- Blow-dryer with cool setting.

For purists who want their wirehaired dogs to look properly wiry and whiskery, the procedure for grooming the wire coat is to strip or pluck it.

Wirehaired Grooming Terminology and Techniques

Wirehaired coats have special grooming terminology and grooming techniques all their own. The wirehaired coat doesn't shed, which is why wirehaired breeds are sometimes good for allergy sufferers. Instead, the hairs grow longer and become looser in the coat, but look unruly and dull in color. The proper way to groom a wirehaired coat is to pluck it or strip it, or do both. Plucking or stripping are methods of removing the hairs by pulling them out with the fingers (plucking) or with a special tool called a stripping knife (stripping). A stripping knife isn't sharp. It simply provides a flat metal surface to grip the hair between the blade and your thumb.

Plucking or stripping the longer, older, duller hairs keeps the skin healthy and stimulated and makes room for newer, brighter hairs to grow in. It keeps the dog looking neat and well groomed, and it's even kind of fun. However, it takes a long time, especially on a large dog.

Your groomer may not do the procedure for you, either, and even if she did, you would probably have to pay dearly because it is so time-consuming. Most wirehaired pet owners are better off learning the technique themselves (or, again, shaving down their pets periodically).

The Stages and Schedules

Wirehaired coats grow in three stages: new growth, old growth, and in-between growth. Keeping these stages in

Keeping your dog in his proper wirehaired coat is a time-consuming job.

Part 3

The Terrier Mitt

The terrier mitt is a special kind of grooming brush that slips over the hand. Designed to stimulate the skin, loosen dead coat, and keep new coat tight and dense, the terrier mitt is perfect for all wirehaired breeds. Although it isn't an absolutely necessary tool, you may find it becomes your favorite grooming item for your wirehaired dog.

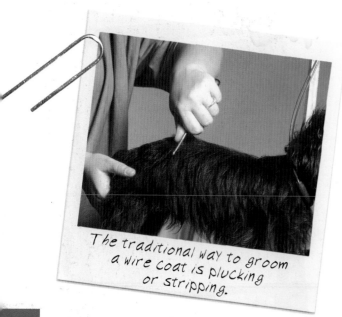

The traditional way to groom a wire coat is plucking or stripping.

Patience Required

If you choose to roll the coat, you won't achieve a full show coat for almost half a year because the gradual removal of old coat results in a gradual replacement with new coat at a much slower rate. Taking the coat all the way down will bring in a bright new show coat in a much shorter time (about two to three months), but it is a lot more work and not necessary for the pet owner.

mind, plucking and stripping can be done on one of two schedules: rolling the coat or taking the coat down.

Rolling the coat means plucking or stripping little bits at a time—a few plucks of hair here and there every day all year round. Rolling the coat leaves some of all three stages of hair in the coat at all times, but diligently removes old coat on a regular basis to keep new growth coming in and to keep color bright.

The other option, and one more commonly practiced by show dog handlers and breeders, is to take the coat all the way down. That means doing a massive plucking or stripping job all at one time to completely remove the old growth in one fell swoop and allow lots of brand-new bright coat to grow in all at once. With the Schnauzer, this is done in stages over a four-week period. Body coat is done the first week, followed by hindquarters, neck, and head. In this manner, the hair grows to the appropriate lengths for the show ring. The undercoat should be stripped after all the hard wire coat is removed.

Plucking or stripping the coat can be done on a continual basis, or all at one time.

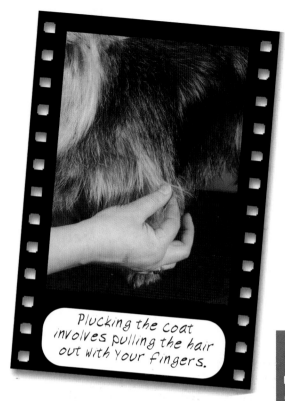

Ouch?

Some people still think plucking is cruel and that shaving the wirehaired coat is the only humane grooming procedure, but nothing could be further from the truth. Done correctly, plucking should not be painful or uncomfortable for your dog. Dog skin is less sensitive and much looser than human skin. It doesn't feel like plucking eyebrows feels to us, so don't be afraid you are hurting your dog.

Plucking the coat involves pulling the hair out with your fingers.

Taking the coat all the way down two to three months before an important dog show can result in a beautiful wiry coat, but for most pet owners who may not even be able to tell the difference, rolling the coat is much easier to practice. Most of us can spare a few minutes each day more easily than an entire afternoon taking down a coat.

For the purposes of this book, we will assume you choose to roll the coat or pluck or strip out small amounts on a regular basis.

Plucking

Plucking the coat is probably the easiest method because you don't have to learn to manipulate the stripping knife, and your only tools are your own two hands—and possibly some grooming powder. Many show dog groomers agree that plucking (sometimes called "hand stripping") is also the superior method, as it targets individual hairs more precisely and can result in a more thorough job. It takes longer than stripping, however, because you will take out fewer hairs with each pull.

Done correctly, plucking is not painful or uncomfortable for the dog.

Part 3

However, if you pull the hair carelessly, straight up, or not in the direction of hair growth, or if you pull without holding the skin taut with your opposite hand, you could irritate your dog, so practice, practice, practice, and always take just a few hairs at a time to keep the procedure pleasant. And don't forget periodic treats to reward your dog for being so patient.

Now, let's get to the plucking procedure. To practice, begin on the back toward your dog's hind end, as this area is easily accessible. To pluck, first hold the skin taut above where you will pluck with your non-dominant hand. If desired, sprinkle a little grooming powder over the area to make the hairs easier to grip. With your dominant hand, grasp just a few hairs (really, just a few) and pull them down and straight out in the direction of hair growth.

Keeping the skin taut will help to keep this procedure painless for your dog, and you'll be better able to see which hairs to pluck. The new growth should stay firmly rooted and the longer, old growth should come out more easily. Once you get the hang of it, you can pluck in a regular fashion, doing a certain area each week, or working your way in a certain pattern to cover all parts of your dog. Here is one suggested method.

1. Begin by plucking from the withers (shoulders) to the base of the tail.

2. Then, pluck from the neck to tail on each side, to cover the entire torso.

3. Scissor around the anal area to keep it free of stray hairs.

4. Remove hair down each leg, then from chest to belly to avoid a skirted appearance (especially in short-legged terriers like Scotties and Westies).

5. Pluck the neck, throat, and head.

6. Remove all long stray hairs from the face and around the eyes.

7. Pluck all long hairs from inside and outside the ears.

Stripping

Stripping with a stripping knife is faster than plucking but may be less precise. When you are pressed for time, however, the stripping knife can be your best friend. The stripping

Straight and Narrow

When plucking or stripping your wirehaired dog's coat, be sure to pull straight out and down in the direction of hair growth. Pulling to the side or up while plucking can actually result in broken hairs and new growth that comes in curly. This is a sure sign of poor grooming in a wirehaired dog. So remember to stay on the straight and narrow!

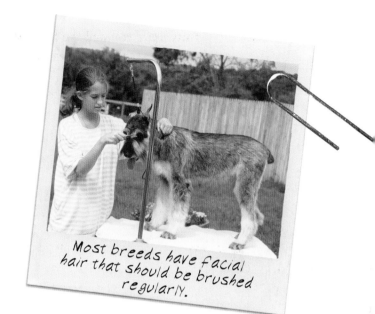

Most breeds have facial hair that should be brushed regularly.

knife looks like a straight comb but with very shallow teeth. It should be very dull, so it doesn't cut off the hairs but instead helps you to pull them from the root. Hold the comb in your dominant hand and catch up a small amount of hair in the comb with your thumb. Pull it out firmly in the direction of coat growth. Don't twist your wrist or pull up, or the hair could break off. Pull it out straight from the root. Work over the coat in the same order as listed above for plucking.

Grooming the Wire Coat

Although plucking or stripping wire coats is essentially the same for all breeds, different breeds within the wire coat category have different shapes and, ultimately, different grooming procedures required in addition to plucking or stripping.

These breeds are all groomed similarly (though not identically) to the Miniature Schnauzer. Some breed fans will be horrified if you groom a long-legged wire breed to look exactly like a Schnauzer, but for many,

Be sure to pull straight out and down in the direction of the hair growth.

Part 3

The Long-Legged Terriers

The long-legged terriers with wire coats include the following breeds:

Airedale Terrier

Border Terrier

Wire Fox Terrier

Irish Terrier

Parson (Jack) Russell Terrier (wirehaired)

Lakeland Terrier

Schnauzer (Miniature, Standard, and Giant)

Welsh Terrier

this clip is practical and easy to maintain. For exact grooming instructions for your breed, consult your national or local breed club or professional show groomer.

The Long-Legged Terriers

Here are basic instructions on how to groom your long-legged wirehaired terrier.

1. Begin with a good, thorough brushing with a natural bristle brush, a slicker brush, and a shedding comb or fine-toothed comb to remove as much loose coat as possible, to stimulate the skin, and to loosen dead coat to make plucking easier.

2. After bathing, blow-dry while brushing until coat is dry.

3. Decide if you want to maintain a stripped dog, or if you want to take the easy route and clip your dog. As mentioned earlier, many pet owners clip their wirehaired dogs because this is an easy and quick way to maintain their pets.

4. If you decide to clip, use a #7, #8, or #10 blade to clip the body coat to approximately one-quarter inch in length. Clip from neck to tail base, clip body sides, and for Schnauzers only, clip half way down rear legs along the back. Leave front legs, belly, and the inside of back legs unclipped.

5. Trim chest hair and underbelly hair with a scissors to neaten and shape as necessary.

6. Shave abdomen/groin area.

7. Shave or clip carefully around the anal area and under tail.

8. Remember to maintain a smooth line from clipped to unclipped portions of the body.

9. Clip or pluck hair from inside and outside ears, and shave or trim to neaten.

10. Clip the head to neaten and shape. Comb and shape eyebrow, beard, and/or

moustache hair (as relevant) forward and neaten to attain the proper head shape for your breed (see the following section).

11. If you decide to pluck or strip, do so according to the instructions above. A major plucking or stripping a couple of times a year when the coat begins to look particularly long and dull (a sign that the coat is "blown") will keep the coat in show condition.

Clipping patterns for the Schnauzer (Giant, shown here, Miniature, or Standard)

Clipping patterns for the Lakeland Terrier

Clipping patterns for the Airedale Terrier

Clipping patterns for the Irish Terrier

Part 3

Rectangular heads should be trimmed to accentuate their beards and protruding eyebrows.

The Terrier Face-Fall

Most wirehaired terriers are groomed with a divided eyebrow, but four wirehaired terriers are groomed with a fall of hair extending across the stop from the crown of the head and about halfway down the muzzle. Here are the four terriers groomed with a fall over the stop.

Kerry Blue Terrier

Lakeland Terrier

Sealyham Terrier

Soft Coated Wheaten Terrier

Heads Up

Wirehaired terriers should have any of three different head shapes when grooming is complete: rectangular, cylindrical, and round.

The rectangular heads contain long, square, angular beards and protruding eyebrows. The terriers with rectangular heads include the Airedale, Lakeland, Scottish, and Sealyham Terriers and the Miniature Schnauzer. The distinctive eyebrows should be trimmed. Start by combing the eyebrow forward, then place the flat side of the scissors beside the outer corner of the eye. Point the blade tip toward the center of the nose and make a straight, smooth cut. The Border Terrier has a wide head, but eyebrows should be removed, and the breed has a natural moustache but no beard.

The Lakeland is one of the terriers that have a distinctive fall of hair.

Cylindrical heads have shorter beards, protruding eyebrows, and a more rounded shape to the crown and muzzle. These include the Wire Fox, Irish, Parson (Jack) Russell, and Welsh Terriers. These heads are trimmed to be narrower and the beards should be somewhat shorter than the typical Schnauzer beard.

Short-Legged Wirehaired Terriers

The short-legged wirehaired terriers include the following:

Australian Terrier

Cairn Terrier

Dandie Dinmont Terrier

Norfolk Terrier

Norwich Terrier

Scottish Terrier

Sealyham Terrier

West Highland White Terrier

The Sealyham's coat is characteristic of a short-legged terrier.

Finally, a handful of terriers have rounded heads with full face furnishings, no beards, and no defined eyebrows. Instead, they have full faces with mane-like furnishings. These include the Australian, Cairn, Dandie Dinmont, Norfolk, Norwich, and West Highland White Terriers.

The Short-Legged Terriers

The short-legged terriers are all groomed similarly (though not identically) to the Scottish Terrier, with the exception of differing head shapes; most of the short-legged wirehaired terriers have round heads, with the exception of the Scottish Terrier and the Sealyham Terrier, with their dramatically rectangular heads.

For exact grooming instructions for your breed, consult your national or local breed club or professional show groomer.

Here are basic instructions on how to groom your short-legged wirehaired terrier.

1. Begin with a good, thorough brushing with a natural bristle brush, a slicker brush, and a shedding comb or fine-toothed comb to remove as much loose coat as possible, to

stimulate the skin, and to loosen dead coat to make plucking easier.

2. After bathing, blow-dry while brushing until coat is dry.

3. Decide if you want to maintain a stripped dog, or if you want to take the easy route and clip your dog. As mentioned earlier, many pet owners clip their wirehaired dogs because this is an easy and quick way to maintain their pets.

4. If you decide to clip, use a #5, #7, or #8 blade to clip the body coat to approximately one quarter of an inch in length.

5. Clip from neck to tail base and about halfway down the tail, blending clipped hair into unclipped.

6. Clip body sides to about the level of the first leg joint so that the clipped area extends in a straight line from front to back, parallel to the floor. To avoid a hula skirt look, blend clipped area into unclipped area.

7. Clip chest from under the muzzle to about one inch above the breastbone.

8. Leave front legs, belly, and the inside of back legs unclipped.

9. Trim chest hair and underbelly hair with a scissors to neaten and shape as necessary.

10. Shave abdomen/groin area.

11. Shave or clip carefully around the anal area and under tail.

12. Remember to maintain a smooth line from clipped to unclipped portions of the body.

13. Clip or pluck hair from inside and outside ears and shave or trim to neaten.

14. Clip the head to neaten and shape. Comb and shape eyebrow, beard, and/or moustache hair (as relevant) forward and neaten to attain the proper head shape for your breed (see the previous section).

15. If you decide to pluck or strip, do so according to the instructions above. A major plucking or stripping a couple of times a year when the coat begins to look particularly long and dull (a sign that the coat is "blown") will keep the coat in show condition.

No-Terrier Zone

Not every wirehaired dog is a terrier, even though these are the breeds people most often picture with wiry coats. Wirehaired breeds appear in every group except Non-Sporting, and

Cairn Terrier

Scottish Terrier

Sealyham Terrier

West Highland White Terrier

while every wirehaired breed *can* be stripped or plucked, each breed within the following groups has individual grooming requirements. Let's go over them group by group.

Sporting

This group includes the gun dogs with wire coats; the German Wirehaired Pointer and the Wirehaired Pointing Griffon.

For the German Wirehaired Pointer, after bathing and drying, pluck the coat with your fingers or a stripping knife. Keep the face clipped to about 1.5 inches, but leave the beard and eyebrows. Pluck longer hairs from body and legs. Or clip body and head with #7 blade on an electric clipper, but leave hair on ribcage and underside of legs, and leave beard and eyebrows.

For the Wirehaired Pointing Griffon, leave the coat in its natural, unkempt, medium length. Pluck or clip only on the ears, top of head, cheeks, and feet. Leave the rest of the coat in its natural state, but brush frequently to remove dead coat. This breed should have a prominent mustache and eyebrows but not a beard.

Hound

The wirehaired hound breeds are distinguished by their natural look. As a rule, these breeds shouldn't

The Wirehaired Pointing Griffon's coat should be kept in its natural state.

Land of the Wire Coat

Have you noticed that a large number of the wire-coated breeds come from the British Isles? The weather-resistant wire coat is particularly helpful for enduring the harsh, wet climate of the British Isles and for doing the work required of so many of the British breeds: outdoor farm work such as herding sheep and controlling vermin.

be trimmed or shaped in any way, but they should be brushed and combed thoroughly and periodically plucked or stripped to keep the coat clean and bright. This group includes the following: the wirehaired Dachshund, Irish Wolfhound, Otterhound, Petit Basset Griffon Vendeen (PBGV), and the Scottish Deerhound.

The wirehaired Dachshund may require some neatening of his beard, and the underbelly hair may need a bit of trimming, but other than that, roll these coats or brush and comb them thoroughly and you will find they are pretty easy to care for. Keep the Otterhound and the PBGV brushed often to prevent mats, as these coats are longer and dense. The biggest challenge with the Irish Wolfhound and the Scottish Deerhound is their sheer size.

Working

The Giant and Standard Schnauzers are officially working breeds, but they should be groomed exactly like the Miniature Schnauzer, as described above in the long-legged terrier section.

Toy

The two wirehaired toy breeds are the Affenpinscher and the Brussels Griffon.

These little fellows are small, so they are relatively easy to hand strip, and they should be kept in a natural coat unshaped by an electric clipper. Trim extra hair between foot pads, neaten ears, and pluck a few areas evenly around the coat every day, and your little toy dog will look as feisty as any terrier.

Herding

The Bouvier des Flandres is the notable wirehaired herding breed. Similar in look to a Giant Schnauzer, the Bouvier should be groomed in a similar manner. Dry the thick, heavy coat, comb with a steel comb, shave ears with a #10 blade from base to tip, and hand strip the face, leaving

The toy breeds with wire coats are generally easy to groom.

The Bouvier des Flandres should be kept in the same manner as a Schnauzer.

tall erect eyebrows and a wide, thick beard. This is time consuming because the Bouvier is such a large dog, but the Bouvier head should not be clipped.

Scissor around the anal area and feet to neaten but leave the rest of the coat natural, as it is designed to protect against harsh weather conditions and is characteristic of the breed. If you really would rather keep your Bouvier in a shorter coat, you can clip the body down with and #7 or #5 blade in the way you would clip a Schnauzer. The Bouvier is prone to sunburn if clipped too short, so be careful.

Grooming the Curly or Wavy Coat

Finally, we come to the curly coat–the most famous of grooming challenges, and the coat worn by that most famously groomed of breeds, the Poodle. Curly or wavy coats aren't always difficult to maintain, depending on what you decide to do with them. Keeping a standard Poodle in constant, full show regalia is practically a full-time job, while your marcelled American Water Spaniel or corded Puli won't require nearly the time investment. Yet even these breeds take time and care to maintain a show-quality coat.

Because of the challenging nature of the curly/wavy coat, many pet owners decide to keep their curly-coated pets clipped down in an

Grooming the curly coat can be most challenging.

Every wavy or curly-coated breed has a unique coat with different requirements.

Practice Makes Perfect

To really master the grooming of a curly-coated breed—especially scissoring the curly coat into a correct shape—you need to practice, and practice, and practice! Clipping and scissoring to shape a curly coat isn't easy. The key is to closely study the breed standard and grooming requirements for your individual breed. Always keep a picture of a well-groomed example available and talk to groomers, breeders, and handlers about the best grooming techniques for your curly-coated breed. One good thing about curly coats is that they grow back. Your Poodle is an ever self-correcting canvas for your continued grooming practice, so if you don't get those cuffs scissored perfectly, you'll have another chance next month.

easy-care pet clip. Even so, many of the curly-coated breeds (particularly the Poodle, the Bichon, and the terriers) require a certain amount of shaping and trimming to match the breed standard, so they will have the look of their breed. A monthly trip to the groomers or even a monthly wielding of the clippers at home will keep curly coats under control.

When in doubt, pets can *always* be cut down without compromising the curly coat. The key is to keep these breeds brushed, combed, and tangle-free.

Curly coats tangle and knot easily. They also tend to be dry and should always be sprayed with a coat dressing, oil spray, or some water with conditioner or cream rinse mixed in before brushing; brushing a dry coat will result in breakage.

For most pet owners, keeping the coat trimmed to a manageable length of a couple inches is by far the most practical solution. Even in relatively easy-care coats, however, the wavy and curly-coated breeds still require lots of grooming, and, even at a short length, should not usually be brushed without a protective spray of conditioner or oil applied first.

To groom your wavy or curly-coated dog, have the following tools ready:

- Pin brush

- Natural bristle brush

- Slicker brush

- Combination medium/fine-toothed metal comb

- Shedding comb

- Scissors, for shaping and trimming

- Electric clippers with a variety of blade sizes as relevant for breed, for shaping and keeping anal area clean.

- Coat dressing or coat oil spray.

The curly-coated breeds fall naturally into several categories: the sporting/water breeds, the herding breeds, the terriers, and the companion breeds. Let's look in more detail at how to groom your curly-coated dog by beginning with a look at this unique coat type.

Curls, Cords, Waves, and Marcels

Just like some humans are blessed (or cursed, depending on your point of view) with ringlets, waves, and a tendency to frizz, some breeds of dogs sport curly or wavy coats. Some of these breeds have single coats that continue to grow like human hair and some have double coats with wooly undercoats. While the undercoated curls tend to mat more quickly, all curly and wavy coats, by their very nature, are prone to mat because the hairs curl back on themselves and knot easily.

Curly-Coated Breeds

Every wavy or curly-coated breed has differing requirements for its unique coat, but they all share certain characteristics, too. The curly-coated breeds include the following:

American Water Spaniel

Bedlington Terrier

Bichon Frise

Curly-Coated Retriever

Irish Water Spaniel

Kerry Blue Terrier

Komondor

Poodle (Standard, Miniature, and Toy)

Portuguese Water Dog

Puli

Part 3

Electric clippers are useful for shaping and keeping the curly coat neat.

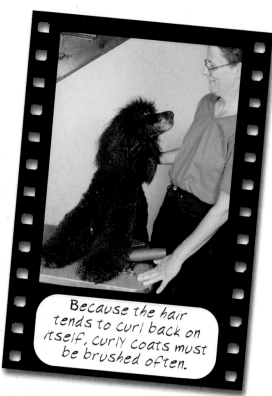

Because the hair tends to curl back on itself, curly coats must be brushed often.

All Wet

You may notice the term "water" in several of the curly-coated breeds. Indeed, the curly coat is particularly good at insulating and repelling water, and even the Poodle was originally a water retriever, although today it is mostly used as a companion. (Some people even argue that the Poodle should be classified as a Sporting breed!) Other breeds, such as the herding and terrier breeds, probably benefited from their curly coats as they worked out in the harsh, wet elements; the curly coats protected against rain, keeping the dog warm and relatively dry.

For this reason, all curly coats must be brushed and combed—and often! The exception is the corded coat, which should be teased out with the fingers to encourage the natural, mat-free cord formation. Also, for breeds with crisp curls like the Irish Water Spaniel, wash and shape without brushing during the drying process to keep the curls intact.

The Water Breeds

The water breeds are sporting dogs with harsh curly coats. Because these dogs typically spend a lot of time out in the field, retrieving from water, flushing upland game, and serving as all-purpose hunting companions, their coats should be kept short and neat. Long, straggly curls will latch onto every stray twig, burr, and piece of underbrush they come into contact with.

Show coats are scissored into a neat shape, and this precise scissoring of the curly coat is labor-intensive. Those who keep curly-coated sporting breeds for hunting and as pets are much more likely to clip them down with an electric clipper to a length of about 2 inches (with the exception of the Curly-Coated Retriever, whose coat is short enough that it doesn't require clipping).

Part 3

Here is how to groom your wavy or curly-coated sporting breed.

1. Before bathing, brush out the entire coat with a pin brush and/or slicker brush to remove as much dead coat as possible and to de-tangle. Tackle mats with a mat comb or coat rake, or cut through them with a scissors to remove (see Chapter 15 for more on how to remove a mat).

2. Run a comb through the entire coat to be sure you removed every tangle.

3. Scissor the leg hair evenly, removing excess hair.

4. Cut hair from under the foot and between the foot pads. The foot should appear rounded and should blend in with the leg hair, appearing like a powder puff over the foot.

Cut hair from under the foot so that the foot appears rounded and blends with the leg.

5. Clip down torso to 2 inches, or scissor off fuzz and shape by scissoring the sides to neaten. Shape the sides and rear to best match the shape of the breed. An imperfect form can be slightly adjusted by the shape in which you trim the curly coat. Take off just a little at a time, periodically standing back to examine the shape of the dog and to compare it to a picture of a well-groomed specimen of your breed.

6. After the bath, do not blow-dry or brush the body coat. Let the curls, waves, or marcels air-dry naturally so they stay intact.

In addition, each of the individual sporting breeds with curly or wavy coats require certain individual adjustments, even for pets.

American Water Spaniel

The American Water Spaniel's close, curly or marcelled coat can be kept trimmed short or scissored to shape. This breed has more feathering on the tail and legs than the Irish Water Spaniel, but is otherwise groomed in a similar fashion. Trim feathers on the underside of

The Irish Water Spaniel should have a peaked topknot and a natural beard.

The Portuguese Water Dog is usually shown in one of two clips: the Retriever clip or the Lion clip.

the tail to neaten into a sickle shape and to remove stray long hairs, but in general, leave the outline of this breed so it is natural. Be sure to keep those flowing ears tangle-free!

Curly-Coated Retriever

The Curly-Coated Retriever has a short coat of crisp curls that requires very little trimming and needn't be shaved down. Brush and comb through before the bath, and remove any stray longer hairs all over the head and body with a scissors. Bathe and don't touch the coat. Allow it to air-dry, unbrushed.

Irish Water Spaniel

The Irish Water Spaniel should have a peaked topknot and a beard left in place. You can shape the topknot with the scissors into a peak between the eyes, removing stray or uneven hairs. Shave the face smooth in the direction of hair growth, or scissor to neaten. This breed also has a characteristic "rat tail"–a long, thin tail with very short hair. Curls at the tail base should blend gradually into the tail but shouldn't extend more than about three inches down the tail. Keep the topknot and ears tangle-free.

Portuguese Water Dog

This breed doesn't shed but grows its hair-coat just like human hair, necessitating regular brushing and haircuts. The Portuguese Water Dog typically sports one of two clips: the Retriever clip, in which it is shaved down to about one inch all over with the tail tuft left long; or the Lion clip (the clip most often seen in the show ring) in which the hindquarters (except for the tail tip) are clipped short, but the forequarters–chest, back, front legs, and head–are left long and wavy or curly, depending on the coat.

The Retriever clip is certainly the easiest to care for. If you choose to keep your Portuguese Water Dog in a Lion clip, comb or pick out tangles all the way to the skin at least every other day.

The Herding Breeds

The herding breeds with curly coats are typically allowed to form corded coats. Any long-haired, curly-coated dog has the potential to form cords (like "dreadlocks") and Poodles were once shown this way, but today, the two breeds most known for sporting corded coats are the large white Komondor and the small black Puli.

Thick cords need grooming so that the cords develop without matting.

Corded coats are easy to groom once cords have formed, normally by two years of age. To facilitate cord formation, work out mats and wooly tangles with the fingers so the coat will cord without matting. Here is how to groom a corded dog.

1. Do not brush or comb out the corded coat!

2. Shave the anal area carefully to a half-inch and shave the abdomen from groin to naval and down the insides of both thighs.

3. While bathing, use a sponge to work water and then shampoo into the cords. Rinse thoroughly.

4. Squeeze-dry cords with a towel.

5. Trim and neaten frayed ends with scissors.

6. To remove mats, use a mat-splitting comb and reshape cords by hand.

Shave down the abdomen, legs, feet, and anal area of your corded dog to keep them clean.

Part 3

Curly Terriers

The Bedlington and Kerry Blue Terriers are uniquely curly terriers with soft coats, so unlike the wirehaired terriers, they don't require stripping. Instead, these breeds are scissored for the show ring, although pets may be clipped with an electric clipper.

Bedlington Terrier

To achieve the Bedlington Terrier's characteristic lamblike look:

1. Using a #15 blade, shave the face from the front edge of the ears to the outer eye corners and straight down to a half-inch from the corner of the mouth, including underjaw, against the direction of hair growth.

2. Shave the back edges of the ears diagonally down to a point at the base of the throat and down to about 2 inches below the Adam's apple in a V-shape.

3. Clip ears on both sides, leaving a V-shaped tassle at the end of both ears.

4. Carefully shave the anal area, and shave the underside of the tail about one third of the way down, then shave the rest of the tail on all sides.

5. The rest of the body should be shaved (for pets) or scissored to about 1 inch all around.

6. The leg hair should be clipped or scissored to be slightly longer than the body hair. Trim between foot pads and scissor around the feet to emphasize their angular "hare foot" shape.

7. Finally, scissor the topknot of the Bedlington so it forms a "Roman arch" or "Roman nose" from the base of the neck to the tip of the nose, to achieve the characteristic lamb look.

Clipping patterns for the Bedlington Terrier

Kerry Blue Terrier

The Kerry Blue Terrier has an overall shape similar to the Wire Fox Terrier, but the coat is soft and wavy rather than hard and wiry. To groom a Kerry Blue Terrier:

1. Clip the stomach with a #10 blade to about 3 inches in front of the back legs. Carefully clip the ears on both sides.

Clipping patterns for the Kerry Blue Terrier

2. On the head, imagine a line from behind the ears to the upper chest and another line from just between the eyes to the hair follicle lump under the chin, shaving under the jaw into a V-shape on the chest that comes to about 2 inches above the breastbone.

3. Comb beard hair forward and carefully cut hair around the eyes with a scissors.

4. Scissor or shave the body coat to about 1.5 inches with a #5 or #7 blade on the clipper. Trim tail hair short and shave the anal area. Shave hair between these lines including the top of the skull, then blend with a scissors into the beard and muzzle.

5. Brush leg hair with a slicker brush and trim feet to a cylindrical shape.

6. Finish by top-brushing the coat with a natural bristle brush sprayed with coat conditioner for a nice sheen.

Curly Companions

The final category of curly-coated dogs is the companion category: the Bichon Frise and the Poodle. Both these breeds require constant vigilance to keep their ever-growing coats free of mats and tangles. Never bathe a matted Poodle or Bichon. Instead, spray these curly coats with coat conditioner and brush and comb them *every day* to keep them untangled. Treat these coats with care to avoid hair breakage.

Part 3

The Bichon's distinctive head is round and should be scissored accordingly.

Bathe your curly companion every two to four weeks and rinse thoroughly. After towel-drying, blow-dry with a slicker or pin brush, brushing away from the body to achieve a fluffy, powder puff appearance.

Though the Bichon and Poodle coats are similar in texture, Poodles may be cut into many different styles. Bichons are typically cut into one characteristic style, resembling a powder puff.

Bichon Frise

To shape the Bichon, think *round*. Keep eyeing a picture of a well-groomed Bichon as you work, scissoring rather than clipping to shape the Bichon coat. Here's how.

1. After bathing and fluff-drying, face your Bichon and comb topknot off face. Scissor off any hair covering the eyes.

2. Part hair on the muzzle and scissor off hair blocking vision. Comb muzzle hair down.

3. Scissor the top of the head into a rounded shape, blending head hair into ears and beard to form a half-moon shape.

4. Neaten but do not shorten the beard.

5. Trim hair under ears so ears fall naturally.

6. Round the head from profile. Keep scissoring to achieve a round shape.

7. Blend chest hair into beard, neck, and head to continue the rounded lines.

8. Scissor front legs into straight lines from the front, cylindrical from afar.

9. Trim hair between the legs to blend into the bottomline from the side.

10. Trim topline level, with coat along the back shorter than on the neck.

11. Leave tail hair long but neaten and shorten around the anal area.

Poodle (Standard, Miniature, and Toy)

At last we come to the Poodle, the breed most likely to appear in the widest variety of grooming styles. The Poodle's versatile coat suits it for an endless number of clips. The Poodle may have a clean, shaved face, a rounded moustache, a squared-off French moustache, and any number of different body styles.

In the showring, any Poodle under 12 months may be shown in a "Puppy" clip, but all adult Poodles must be shown in either the English Saddle clip or the Continental clip. Pet Poodles are characteristically kept in short, easy-care coats but require clipping about every four weeks.

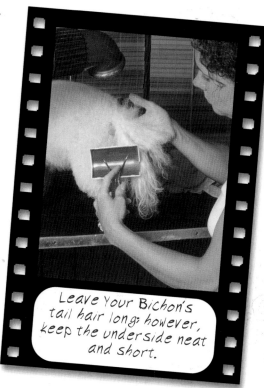

Leave your Bichon's tail hair long; however, keep the underside neat and short.

The fun thing about Poodles is that you can easily try different styles and clips. That coat grows so fast that it lends itself to experimentation. Whether you decide to clip your Poodle yourself or a let a professional groomer do it, keep your Poodle well brushed and combed between clipper sessions to keep that curly coat from becoming a mess of mats.

Poodles can be clipped into many different styles. Some of the coat options available include the following:

• Puppy clip

• English saddle clip

• Continental clip

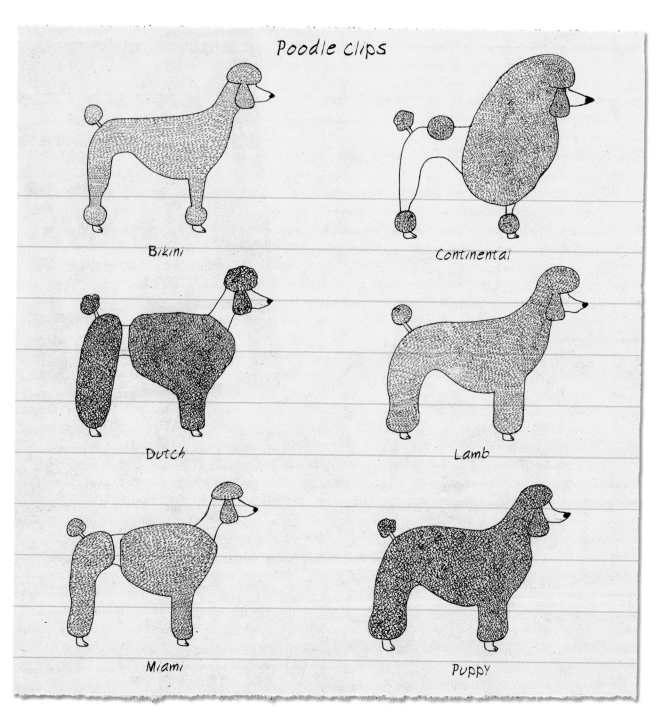

Poodle Clips

Bikini

Continental

Dutch

Lamb

Miami

Puppy

Poodle clips

Town and Country

Sporting

Teddy Bear

Retriever

New Yorker

English Saddle

Part 3

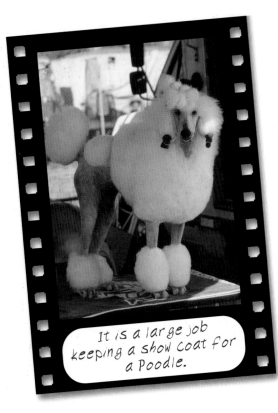

It is a large job keeping a show coat for a Poodle.

- Sporting clip

- Lamb clip

- Retriever clip

- Miami clip

- Town and country clip

- Teddy bear clip

- New Yorker clip

- Dutch clip

- Kennel clip

- Bikini clip

Maintaining a show coat on a Poodle is an awesome task. Topknot and ears are banded and wrapped to keep them clean, and the coat is handled with immaculate care in order not to break the hairs and compromise the coat's quality. For the pet owner, however, a shorter and more sensible clip is much easier to maintain. Even so, keep a picture of the clip you are imitating in front of you so you can keep checking the shape and comparing it to your work.

Bathe your Poodle every two to four weeks. Then, to groom him at home in a basic Kennel clip:

1. Fluff dry the coat with a soft slicker brush and a blow-dryer set on low or cool.

2. Shave the face with a #15 blade on an electric clipper. Or, leave a doughnut-shaped or French moustache on the muzzle, shaping with a scissors.

3. The Poodle is the only breed with feet shaved clean. This is difficult and must be practiced carefully, especially on Toy Poodles with tiny feet. With the same #15 blade, clip the paws on the top, sides, between the toes, and between the pads.

4. Clip the tail, leaving a pom-pom (shaped with a scissors) on the end of the tail, if desired.

5. Shave the body with a #5 blade down the backbone from the base of the neck to the base of the tail, then down each side, including chest and ribs, to about a half-inch in length. Blend the neck into the coat.

6. Scissor the legs to about half-inch in length.

7. Brush and comb out long ear hair, trimming with a scissors to neaten.

8. Shape the topknot by scissoring the headpiece into a rounded shape.

9. Next month, experiment with a different clip.

Finally, remember that even with regular professional grooming, curly coats need brushing and combing, all the way to the skin, every day (or almost every day).

A basic clip is best for the pet Poodle.

Part 3

Part Four

Grooming for Special Needs

"Save it, Marty. I told you conditioners were no good for our hair type"

Grooming a Puppy

Puppies may be small–or relatively small–but those squirming, wagging, romping bundles of energy are anything but easy to groom. Puppies love to be on the move, and they may not be particularly thrilled about sitting nicely for a long session of brushing, toenail clipping, and primping. However, because puppies grow, and some grow really big, puppyhood is the best time to establish a regular grooming routine. Just try to trim a full-grown Irish Wolfhound's nails if he doesn't want you to do it. Don't expect to have the upper hand when it comes to physical strength.

Grooming a puppy isn't exactly like grooming an adult dog. Puppy coats are often different than

Puppyhood is the best time to establish a grooming routine.

their adult manifestations will be. Long coats haven't reached their full adult length. Other coat types take a while to achieve their adult texture, their double-coated nature, or their mature fullness. Puppies may not need to be groomed as often as adults, but especially for long and curly-coated breeds that will require frequent grooming as adults, getting puppies in the habit now is the best and easiest way to facilitate future grooming sessions.

The Importance of Socialization

Puppies have certain natural behaviors (barking, jumping, chewing, using the world as their personal toilet) that make socialization and training necessary if they are to live with humans. Training sets up house rules, while socialization is the process of getting a puppy used to lots of different people, other dogs, and diverse situations from a young age so he becomes a well-adjusted, confident, friendly adult dog. Some trainers recommend introducing your puppy to new people, dogs, and situations every single day of his life for the first year.

Socialize Your Puppy to Grooming

Puppies have certain natural tendencies that can make grooming difficult. They may not like their paws handled, they may not be patient enough to stand still for a long detangling session, and they may balk at the handling of their mouths and ears. However, puppies can learn early that grooming is safe, inevitable, and even rewarding.

You can socialize your dog to grooming much in the same way you socialize him to the world in general—simply by exposing him to the grooming process a little bit each day.

Baby Steps

Your puppy is a baby, and just like any young, immature mammal, he must learn things in little steps. You can't expect a 12-week-old Afghan puppy to endure three hours of brushing—and, luckily, the

A puppy's energetic attitude and activity level can make him difficult to groom.

Afghan puppy's coat doesn't yet require it. But someday, that coat will require long hours of grooming, so baby steps are the key to success.

Begin grooming your puppy as soon as you bring him home, and while you can certainly adapt a grooming schedule to fit your own needs, this one works well. Don't rush anything. Whenever your puppy gets nervous or apprehensive about anything you are doing, stop and take it back a step. Little bits of grooming applied consistently, evolving gradually and comfortably into a full-blown grooming routine, will keep grooming positive for both you and your puppy.

Do each of the following activities with your puppy every day at the same time:

Week One

1. Pick up each of your puppy's paws. Wiggle nails and press on paw pads. Give your puppy lots of praise and a small treat or piece of kibble after each paw.

2. Handle each ear and look in the ear. Praise and treat.

3. Touch your puppy's muzzle. Praise and treat.

4. Look at each eye, stroking his face with your hands. Praise and treat.

5. Lift up and handle tail, checking anal area for cleanliness.

> ## Know Your Dog
>
> Every dog is an individual, and knowing how fast you can progress with grooming is a matter of paying attention to the cues your dog delivers. Some tend to adapt quickly to grooming, while others tend to be particularly shy of grooming tools, especially electronic ones. Cowering, whimpering, backing away, urination, or running away are all signs that your shy, sensitive, submissive, or extra-cautious dog is scared or just a little wary of a tool or a grooming process. If this happens, back up and take it extra slow. If your confident dog has no problem with a nail clipping and thorough brushing and combing in that first week, that's fine, too. It's all a matter of adapting to the needs of your dog's individual personality.

Gradually get your puppy used to grooming by touching and petting him on a daily basis.

Part 4

Soon your puppy will let you touch his ears, teeth, and eyes without fussing.

6. Stroke his coat with your hand and praise him.

7. Finish with a treat. Wasn't that fun? (Your puppy surely thought so!)

Week Two
1. Continue Week One items.

2. Gently take your puppy's muzzle in one hand and insert your fingers in the corners of his mouth. Gently touch a couple of teeth with your finger. Praise and treat.

3. Let your puppy sniff and explore a soft natural bristle brush. Put a treat on the bristles for your puppy to find.

4. Let your puppy sniff and explore a nail clipper appropriately sized for your puppy. Praise and offer a treat.

Week Three
1. Continue Week One items.

2. Open your puppy's mouth and rub teeth briefly with a soft cloth. Examine teeth and gums. Try to stop *before* your puppy begins to resist.

3. Gently brush puppy's coat for a few seconds, then praise and treat.

4. Touch the nail clippers against your puppy's paw. If he reacts positively, clip off just the very tip of just one or two nails. Praise and treat.

Week Four
1. Continue Week One items.

2. Let your puppy explore a toothbrush, sniffing and even chewing it a bit. Praise and treat.

3. Put a little toothpaste made for dogs on your finger and allow your puppy to lick it off.

(Don't force it. If he doesn't like it, that's fine. The point is to get him used to the taste, not necessarily to want to gobble it up.)

4. Brush the coat more thoroughly, praising as you go.

5. Clip off any toenail tips you didn't clip last week–just one or two per day.

Week Five

1. Continue Week One items.

2. Touch the toothbrush against your puppy's teeth, scrubbing just a little if your puppy responds well. Praise and treat.

3. Brush coat, then introduce your puppy to a comb. Let puppy sniff it, and touch it on your puppy's coat, combing a little if he responds well.

4. Keep handling paws, monitoring daily and snipping off nail tips when necessary. Don't forget to keep the praise flowing.

Week Six

1. Continue Week One items.

2. Brush your puppy's teeth, briefly. Praise.

3. Brush and comb coat.

4. Continue to handle paws, ears, eyes, tail, and teeth. Be careful handling the mouth when your puppy starts teething. Do not brush the teeth during this time, as the puppy's mouth is extra sensitive.

When introducing the nail clipper, start by clipping just one nail a day.

Treats can help your puppy associate grooming with positive things.

Never underestimate the power of positive reinforcement when introducing grooming to your puppy.

5. Enjoy your well-behaved and well-groomed puppy!

Your puppy should be well socialized to the grooming process by the sixth week. But don't let that be a reason to slack off. Grooming should be a lifelong process, and a little bit every day for life will train your pet to both accept and enjoy the process.

Accentuate the positive. Never underestimate the power of positive reinforcement when training your puppy to do anything. Positive reinforcement works wonders. What puppy wouldn't want to sit nicely for grooming if it means lots of praise, treats, and time with you?

It's easy to take a well-behaved puppy for granted. If grooming sessions become easy, don't let that be an excuse to stop making them fun. Your puppy may begin to backslide, losing interest and patience in grooming, if you start grooming haphazardly or distractedly or forgetting to praise and reinforce your puppy for good behavior.

What to Treat

Big, fattening, artificially colored and flavored, preservative-filled treats aren't good for any dog. To combat obesity and encourage good health, many trainers prefer to use bits of a puppy's regular kibble as a treat. Take kibble from the puppy's regular dietary allowance, rather than adding additional kibble. For example, if your puppy usually gets one cup of kibble a day, feed three-quarters of a cup for meals (divided into two or three meals), and reserve one-quarter cup for treats to use in grooming and training. Every bite counts, especially for toy dogs that can easily become overweight with just a few extra calories each day. Or, try healthy "people food" as a treat: slices of raw baby carrots, blueberries, or tiny broccoli florets. Every now and then, bits of cheese and meat make treats interesting and enjoyable, in addition to adding vitamins. Avoid any treats with artificial colors, flavors, preservatives, and sugar. Nylabone® Edibles are healthy chewing alternatives. Growing puppies don't need junk food any more than growing children need it!

Every grooming session, no matter how old your puppy gets, should end with praise and a treat. Though early grooming sessions will go more smoothly if you give your puppy lots of small treats throughout, grooming doesn't have to become a treat-dispensing session every single time. Those early treats help to associate the grooming process with rewards in your puppy's mind. Once that connection is established, your puppy will enjoy grooming without constant treats.

Also, never underestimate the power of praise. Some puppies, especially those that aren't particularly food-motivated or who can't eat very much at once (small breeds especially), may not care to down too many treats. Overfeeding is never healthy, and considering that obesity is the number-one health problem in pets according to vets, too many treats are never a good idea. Praise can be just as powerful, if not more powerful, than treats, depending on your dog's personality, but a combination of lots of praise and some strategically offered healthy treats works best for most dogs.

Once your puppy gets used to his grooming routine, he will look forward to the time you spend together.

Bonding Time

The daily grooming session does more than teach your puppy how to let you maintain his hygiene. It also allows for built-in one-on-one time for you and your puppy, something crucial to your relationship now and in the future.

It's easy to get busy with daily life and forget to spend time with your puppy. Sure, everyone spends time yelling, "No!" and taking the puppy outside when housetraining seems the central focus of the relationship. After that, it's common to walk that dog and pet him absentmindedly while watching television, but many owners never really spend "quality time" with their pets. No, quality time isn't just for human children–dogs benefit from it, too.

Part 4

Grooming is one chance to focus all your attention on your puppy.

Vet Advice for Home Groomers

The next time you take your puppy to the vet, ask if there are any particular actions your vet would like your puppy to get used to. Tell your vet what you do in a grooming session and see if your vet has anything to add, either in general or as relevant to the health profile of your individual dog. If your vet has an idea, such as massaging sensitive skin or keeping ear hair clipped to prevent infection, incorporate that into your daily routine early in your puppy's life.

When you groom your pet, you are focusing all your attention on him. Talk to him, praise him, give him treats, tell him he is a good dog, and teach him how to let you handle his paws, his face, his ears, his coat. Your dog will learn that he is important to you and that you notice and value him. He will begin to see you as the trusted "pack leader," and his loyalty and devotion will develop quickly. Let grooming time become bonding time and you've accomplished two very important tasks of pet ownership in one short session per day.

The "Pretend" Vet Exam, Step By Step

As if bonding, socializing, and making grooming easier isn't enough, daily puppy grooming sessions accomplish another very important task: They can make your vet's job a lot easier. The puppy grooming session, as mapped out above, gradually introduces a puppy to many of the physical manipulations he would encounter at the veterinarian's office–manipulations that a puppy may not be comfortable with without daily grooming.

During a physical exam, a veterinarian must inspect your puppy's paws and nails, tail and anal area, eyes, ears, muzzle, and teeth. The vet must also be able to palpate the puppy's body, feeling all over the skin and coat to be sure everything is where it should be and that the puppy has no lumps, bumps, areas of irritation, or other abnormalities.

A puppy who is scared of this kind of physical manipulation–one who bites, claws, struggles, yelps, or is otherwise traumatized by a basic examination–is hard to examine properly, and could develop an intense fear of veterinary visits. But the puppy who is socialized to the grooming process, which should include all the poking and prodding a good vet will do, should be easy to examine. Though your puppy may be a little bit nervous being in a new place and meeting a new friend, the examination itself will be old news to the regularly groomed puppy, and that's a good thing for everyone involved.

Addressing Setbacks

Finally, every puppy has setbacks, and every groomer has stories to tell about the Great Dane puppy that was so patient with grooming and then one day suddenly refused to let anyone touch her nails ever again, or the one about the Poodle who wouldn't be seen within a mile of a clipper, or the Shih Tzu who decided she had experienced her very last de-matting session.

Setbacks can occur due to "user error"–clipping the quick on a nail, pulling too hard to untangle a coat, or surprising the dog with an electric clipper before he was prepared. Sometimes, however, setbacks occur for no discernible reason. A puppy is suddenly shy of the scissors, the nail grinder, or even the bathtub and you have no idea why.

When setbacks occur, back up. Take your dog back to the beginning and start over. If your dog suddenly fears nail clipping, go back to that very first stage, when you let your dog explore the nail clippers without actually clipping the nails, rewarding all the while with praise, reassurance, and the occasional treat. Introduce the clipper back, slowly, as if you were socializing the dog to nail clipping for the very first time. Do the same thing with the scissors, clippers, comb, or whatever else your

Getting your puppy accustomed to grooming will also help you when you visit the vet.

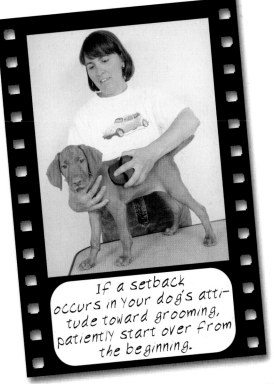

If a setback occurs in your dog's attitude toward grooming, patiently start over from the beginning.

Part 4

As he matures, your dog will lose his puppy coat and grow into his full adult coat.

Don't Blame the Dog!

When your dog has a grooming setback, don't get frustrated and take it out on your dog. Dogs don't suddenly resist nail trimming, clipping, or bathing to annoy you. They resist it because they have a reason to resist it. Something happened—whether or not you know about it or see it from your dog's point of view—to cause your dog to fear or resist some aspect of grooming. Blaming your dog won't help the situation. Patience, consistency, and slow-but-steady progress will bring you both back to your once-happy grooming routine again.

dog balks at. Remember to progress again slowly, with lots of rewards, keeping the experience positive, especially if your dog has had reason to associate grooming with a negative experience. You now have the job of replacing that negative experience with positive experiences again.

Preparing for the Coat's Big Blow

Some puppy coats morph pretty subtly into their adult versions, but some come into their adult coats in a rather dramatic fashion involving tons of hair loss, a temporarily patchy coat, and the development of an undercoat more dramatic and challenging than any the puppy owner had imagined. Some pet owners give up on grooming their pets once that adult coat finally comes in. The Poodle, for instance, experiences a dramatic coat change somewhere around the first birthday, with great changes in both length and thickness. Suddenly, tangles form daily where once they were infrequent.

Knowing a coat change is in the works for your puppy can help you be prepared. Also remember that when your puppy "blows coat" for the first time, losing his puppy coat and growing in his full, thick adult coat, the heavy-duty grooming chores related to the dropped coat won't last forever, and will typically occur only once or twice a year. Just keep brushing, combing, brushing, and bonding!

Parasite Prevention and Treatment

Maybe your dog will be one of the lucky ones who never gets fleas, but don't lay money on it! Fleas aren't just for stray dogs and dogs that live outdoors. Even the most pampered indoor pet can get fleas on a walk or out in the yard. If a dog in the neighborhood or at a dog show has fleas, all pets in the area are at risk.

Any dog who ever walks under a tree or through a wooded area is also at risk for ticks, and any dog who sets foot outside could be bitten by a mosquito. The diseases that fleas, ticks, and mosquitoes carry can threaten the health and even the life of your pet. Lyme disease, tapeworms, heartworm disease, and West Nile virus are just a sampling of the potential hazards from parasites,

Any dog, no matter what his breed or environment, can pick up parasites.

Check your dog's coat for fleas and ticks, especially after playing outside.

Puppy Products

Not all pest control products are designed for puppies. Always read the directions and check with your vet if you are unsure about whether your pest control product of choice is safe for your puppy and appropriate for your puppy's age and weight.

so protecting your pet from parasites is more important now than ever before.

Fortunately, more products are available than ever before to fight fleas, ticks, and mosquitoes. From natural botanicals to the latest in adulticides (which kill adult fleas and ticks), repellents, and various types of insect growth regulators and related substances that keep flea eggs from hatching or even dissolve the shells of fleas and ticks, pest control is advanced, and it continues to advance every year.

For the home groomer, the best course of action is to first determine if you have a pest problem. In areas where pests are a big problem (such as the damp, hot southeastern United States or along the West Coast), prevention can help to curb an inevitable flea infestation when it starts. Using flea control products all year may work best for you.

For other areas of the country, where fleas only pop out for a portion of the year and may not be present in all neighborhoods or environments, it may pay to wait and only use flea control products if you develop a problem, and even to handle minor flea problems with non-chemical means such as frequent bathing and the ever-trusty flea comb. However, the risk in this method is missing the early signs of a flea infestation. The vigilant groomer will detect a problem early–once fleas have a foothold, it can be much harder to get rid of them.

Part 4

Only you can determine how you want to handle pest control for your pet, but this chapter will give you the background and strategies you need to make the right choice for your individual situation.

Grooming = Pest Control

Good grooming establishes the foundation for pest control because a healthy, well-examined coat and strong, healthy skin will help to minimize fleas. Pests are naturally attracted to weak animals with vulnerable skin. Of course, where fleas are prevalent, they will jump onto any host they can find (even humans), but if they have a choice, they will usually infest the less healthy hosts.

A healthy diet and good skin and coat care not only help to discourage a flea infestation, but could help minimize skin reactions to flea and tick bites when they happen. A daily grooming session is also important, especially during flea and tick season. A once-over with a flea comb and careful examination for signs of infestation can alert you to the presence of even a couple of fleas, before they have a chance to multiply.

Flea and Tick Clues

How do you know if fleas are present? Fleas leave telltale signs.

• Flea dirt (digested blood), which looks like tiny, reddish brown specks.

• Flea eggs, which look like tiny white specks.

• Actual fleas, which are brown, about 2 millimeters long, and crawl or jump.

• Itching! Though dogs can itch for many reasons, itching and subsequent scratching is often caused by fleas, especially during warm weather.

Excessive scratching is a sure indication that your dog has a skin problem.

Part 4

How to Remove a Tick

Ticks can transmit a variety of infectious diseases to both dogs and humans, so remove them with caution. Never touch a tick, especially a blood-filled tick, with your bare hands—the bacteria in the blood of the tick could infect you. Also, never pull out a tick with its head buried in your dog's skin, or the wound could become infected. Instead, remove a tick like this.

1. Using a cotton ball, wet the tick with nail polish remover or rubbing alcohol, or with a tick spray available at pet stores.

2. Wait for a few minutes, or until the tick begins to pull out of the skin.

3. Wearing surgical gloves or holding a paper towel, or using tweezers or a special tick-removing tool, lift the tick off your dog.

4. Drop the tick in a small amount of rubbing alcohol. When it is dead, flush it down the toilet.

Ticks are evident by their presence. Ticks can range from pinhead-sized to pea-sized, but when they attach and fill with blood, they can become as large as marbles. You may find them crawling on your dog or attached with their heads buried in your dog's skin.

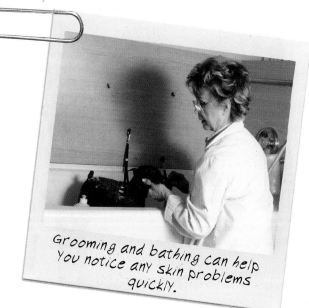

Grooming and bathing can help you notice any skin problems quickly.

The Magic of Water and Comb

For minor pest occurrences, you may not need to do anything more than bathe your dog frequently and use the flea comb diligently. Bathing drowns fleas. You don't even need to use chemicals, although a natural botanical flea dip or shampoo can help repel pests and condition your pet's skin. For dogs that spend time outside, bathe weekly during flea season and finish every grooming session by running through every inch of your dog's coat with a fine-toothed comb, no matter the coat length.

Flea combs remove fleas because the teeth are so close together that they lift the flea from the coat. A daily comb-through with the flea comb between weekly baths will keep many dogs flea-free. However, if more than a flea or two continues to be present daily for more than a week, or if your dog is sensitive to flea bites, consider using a chemical flea control product. Talk to your vet about your best options.

Here's how to rid your dog of fleas, no products required.

1. Bathe your dog in a bathtub or tub of water. Instead of letting the water drain, let the tub fill. Scrub coat well, all the way down to the skin, especially around ears, tails, and abdomen, where fleas tend to congregate.

2. Have your dog sit in the bath water to drown fleas in the tail area as you scrub the rest of the coat.

3. Rinse the coat thoroughly for five minutes, continuously spraying with a hand-held sprayer or pouring clean water from a cup over the entire coat. (Protect ears from getting water in them by plugging with cotton balls or holding the ear, folded over, during rinsing.)

4. Dry as you would normally.

5. Finally, with a flea comb or your dog's regular fine-toothed comb, work slowly over your dog's coat from tail to head. Make sure you comb all the way down to the skin.

6. If any fleas, flea dirt, or flea eggs remain, you'll find them. Drop fleas in a small amount of rubbing alcohol to kill them as you go, then flush them when you are done. You probably won't be able to kill them by squeezing them between your fingers because of their hard shells (and why would you want to?).

7. If you don't find any fleas after the thorough bath, great! However, repeat the flea combing process daily and bathe weekly to keep fleas at bay.

Prevent Infestations Now

For some pets and some environments, bathing and flea combs are not enough. Instead, you need a multi-pronged approach: treat the pet, the house, and in some cases, even the yard. Because there are so many pest control products available, you must decide which kinds you want to use on your pet.

Part 4

There are products you can buy that can help control parasites.

Pest Control for the New Millennium

Old-fashioned flea powders, sprays, dips, and flea collars contain chemicals that must be handled with extreme caution. Preferable are the newer spot-on preparations, which are easy to use and are applied monthly between the pet's shoulder blades and also at the tail base for larger dogs. These chemicals are generally safe for most pets if you follow package directions precisely, but some pets react negatively to these spot-on products. Talk to your vet about which products he or she recommends as safest and most effective for your pet, as there is a variety available for prevention and treatment.

If you are uncomfortable with using the chemicals in flea control products, many of which are neurotoxins, you may decide to use organic products made from natural botanicals and other non-toxic substances. These products don't work as quickly or as thoroughly as mainstream flea and tick control products, but they pose less risk to the pet due to product toxicity or misuse. For serious pest problems, or in areas where fleas and/or ticks are a persistent problem, the most effective product is probably a spot-on product, applied monthly, available from your veterinarian.

Before the advent of spot-ons, which are highly effective at completely controlling fleas in many cases, much more environmental treatment was necessary than it is today. Carpet sprays and powders, room foggers, and yard sprays were once necessary to get a handle on fleas. Still, during flea season, you can help minimize the chances of a flea infestation

Pesticide Caution

Always read directions carefully when using any pesticide for any reason, especially if you have young children. Never use a dog flea product on a cat or vice versa, and always apply the correct dosage at the correct frequency. Talk to your vet if you suspect you may have misused a pesticide, or if your pet experiences any health problems after using a pesticide product, such as rash, hair loss, itching, lethargy, seizures, loss of motor function, or collapse.

by vacuuming frequently (especially areas frequented by your dog) and, in severe cases, sprinkling carpets and furniture with a flea control product made for this purpose (the non-toxic varieties are safest and can be very effective when used in combination with a spot-on product).

Some spot-ons also protect against ticks and/or mosquitoes, so use according to exposure risk.

The Price of Pests

Fleas are more than an inconvenience. They can cause serious health problems for your beloved pet. Here is a rundown of what can happen if your dog develops a pest-related health problem.

From Hot Spots to Hives

Flea, tick, and mosquito bites can irritate even the healthiest of dogs, and dogs with sensitive skin may develop agonizing allergic reactions to flea bites. From flea allergies to fleabite dermatitis, fleas make skin itch. When a dog scratches and licks at one spot too much, the area can become inflamed and infected—a "hot spot." Allergic reactions to flea and tick bites can result in rashes, hives, hair loss, and chronic irritation.

Constant skin irritation can compromise your dog's quality of life, so stop it before it starts, and if your dog does develop a skin irritation or allergy from pests, don't ignore it. See your vet and treat it right away, before it gets worse. Your dog has much better things to do than scratch his life away.

Good nutrition is the first step to a healthy coat.

Your vet can advise you about products and vaccinations that can help protect your pet from pest-borne illnesses.

Pest-Borne Diseases

The most common flea to bite dogs is actually the cat flea (*C. felis*), which lives on blood. Fleas can transmit many diseases to your pet through a flea bite; so can ticks and mosquitoes. The following are some of the flea, tick, and mosquito-borne diseases that affect dogs.

1. Tapeworms, evident via quarter-inch long egg-filled body segments in a dog's feces or around the anal area, are transmitted to dogs through flea bites.

2. Lyme disease, the most common tick-borne illness in the United States (occurring mainly in Northeast, upper Midwest, northern California, and the Pacific Northwest), occurs when a tick bites a dog and stays attached for at least 5 to 20 hours. Humans can also contract Lyme disease from ticks.

3. Rocky Mountain Spotted Fever can be contracted from several tick species; humans can also catch this disease (occurring mainly in the southeastern United States, the Midwest, Plains states, and Southwest).

4. Canine ehrlichiosis, contracted from the common brown dog tick, occurs mainly in the Gulf Coast area, the Eastern seaboard, the Midwest, and California.

5. Tick paralysis is caused by the bite of the female wood tick.

6. West Nile virus is contracted through the bite of an infected mosquito and can infect dogs in the same way it can infect people.

7. Heartworm disease, in which microfilia are spread by mosquitos.

Make pest control a part of your regular grooming routine. Your dog's healthy skin, coat, and maybe even life, are at stake, so don't neglect this crucial aspect of regular grooming.

Part 4

Sensitive Skin Care

A dog's skin is one of his most sensitive and easily damaged organs. Though dogs tolerate puppy biting in the whelping box better than humans tolerate those needle teeth on our hands, dog skin is actually thin and more prone to problems than human skin. If a dog develops a skin problem–an allergy, a wound, or a reaction to a flea bite, for example–it can initiate a cycle of skin problems that can be very difficult to resolve. For this reason, home groomers must take extra care not to aggravate a dog's skin with a hot pair of clippers, a poorly aimed scissors, or too-rigorous brushing with the sharp wire bristles of a slicker brush.

Some breeds in particular have extra sensitive

Some breeds have very sensitive skin and require special handling.

skin and may react to things other breeds would tolerate without a problem. For each individual dog, there is a line between frequent grooming to stimulate the skin and coat, to keep it healthy, to distribute coat oils, and to remove tangles, and over-grooming to the point of aggravating the skin.

Every dog can be brushed and combed daily, but some dogs may need a softer brush or a gentler touch. If your dog has sensitive skin, this chapter is for you, but even pet owners whose dogs seem to have tough, resilient skin can benefit from a little extra caution. Once an irritated skin cycle begins, it can be hard to stop, and you can't reason with a dog about why he shouldn't scratch and lick that itchy, sore spot.

Sensitive Skin: Who Has It?

Any dog can have sensitive skin, but some breeds tend to have more sensitive skin than others. If your dog has a white or light-colored coat and pink skin, a very sparse coat or no coat, he may be more sensitive to everything: dry air, wind, sun, and irritation from products such as shampoos, conditioners, and coat sprays. Some breeds that may tend to have more sensitive skin, ranging from allergies to sunburn risk to skin fold dermatitis, include the following:

Afghan Hound

Basset Hound

Bichon Frise

Boston Terrier

Bulldog

Chinese Crested

Chinese Sharpei

Cocker Spaniel

Dogs with short coats are more likely to have reactions to certain products.

Dalmatian

English Springer Spaniel

French Bulldog

Golden Retriever

Great Pyrenees

Italian Greyhound

Komondor

Manchester Terrier

Pekingese

Pembroke Welsh Corgi

Pug

Saint Bernard

Saluki

Tibetan Terrier

West Highland White Terrier

Whippet

Poodle (white)

Labrador Retriever (yellow)

Light dogs, like the Yellow Lab, may be more susceptible to skin allergies or conditions.

Part 4

Many dogs can develop food allergies that manifest in their skin or coat.

That's not to say that every pink-skinned or light-coated individual will have sensitive skin, or that your black Lab *won't* have sensitive skin. An injury or a flea infestation can cause any dog to develop skin problems. But for those breeds with sensitive skin, take extra care to proceed gently so as not to aggravate the skin.

Special Concerns for Sensitive Skin Grooming

When grooming any dog, take care not to injure the skin. Slicker brushes, clippers, and scissors are all potentially injurious to a dog's skin. For dogs with sensitive skin, use tools lightly, and take special care when grooming a dog with skin problems.

Skin problems are for a vet to address, and a groomer shouldn't try to "fix" these problems, but grooming can certainly prevent some of these problems. Skin disorders that can be caused by or aggravated by grooming include the following.

Watch the Scissors!

One of the most treacherous of grooming activities is scissoring. Some dogs require scissoring to maintain coat shape (such as Poodles and Bichons), and that can mean relatively long sessions with a sharp scissors next to your dog's sensitive skin. Always pay attention when scissoring your dog, and don't turn on the television or have people in the room distracting you. Keep the scissors pointed down, and always err on the side of scissoring too far from the skin rather than too near. It's too easy to miss and cause a laceration—many dogs have visited the vet to have a scissors slice sutured! Even a professional groomer can get distracted and accidentally nick a dog, and a painful event like this can turn your dog off grooming for good, so be careful.

Allergies

Many dogs develop allergies–from food, external environ-mental sources, or inhaled substances. In dogs, allergies are most likely to manifest on the skin. The most common type of allergy in dogs is flea allergy dermatitis, an allergic reaction to flea saliva. Allergies can develop as rashes, hives, and/or severe itching. Don't brush over rashes or hives. If hair is tangled, work through gently with a comb.

Allergies can trigger a vicious cycle–they cause itching, which causes scratching and licking, which causes more irritation. Even after fleas are eliminated, the negative effects on a dog's skin can last for months. Always address allergic reactions with a veterinarian, who can advise you about how to groom hair over these areas.

Brush Burn and Clipper Burn

These skin conditions are a direct result of grooming. Brush burn is caused by brushing too hard, damaging the skin. Clipper burn is a result of allowing a clipper to become too hot (this happens with extended use), burning the dog. Not only can such grooming mishaps be prevented, but when they occur, they can also make future grooming sessions extremely difficult. Dogs remember!

Always brush gently, especially with a wire slicker brush, which can be sharp. Short, gentle strokes are better than long, hard ones to work out tangles. When brushing vigorously down to the skin, use a natural bristle brush and save the slicker brush for working out mats. Also use caution with pin brushes.

Turn off the clipper frequently during grooming, have spare blades handy when the blades you are using get too hot, or use a cooling spray for your clipper. Touch the clipper blade frequently to make sure it isn't too hot. Never run clippers over sensitive areas, like the chin and neck, more than twice, especially when using a #10 or #15 blade.

Brush or clipper burn can occur while grooming, so always be gentle with your dog's sensitive skin.

Part 4

Some shampoos or medications can cause adverse reactions in certain dogs.

How Shakespearean!

The "Elizabethan collar" is a large, round, plastic, cone-shaped collar that surrounds your dog's head so he can't lick or bite his skin. Though most dogs don't enjoy wearing this device, it is sometimes necessary when a dog can't help irritating a wound or other skin problem.

Hot Spots

Hot spots are moist, hot wound-like areas that develop quickly and are very painful. They may be caused by a variety of triggers: fleas, allergies, irritants, infections, even a lack of adequate grooming. Hot spots develop and grow because the dog obsessively licks and scratches at the itchy, painful spots, making it progressively worse until it becomes infected. Vets must treat hot spots and will clip hair away to disinfect and treat the area. The dog will probably be treated for itching and may have to wear an "Elizabethan collar" to prevent irritating the hot spot while it heals.

Parasitic and Fungal Conditions

Fleas and ticks aren't the only creatures that can infect your dog's skin. A fungus can cause ringworm, and a variety of different mites can infect your dog with different kinds of mange. Parasitic and fungal conditions must be treated with medication prescribed by your vet.

Dogs can pick up diseases from other dogs, so be sure that your pup's friends are healthy.

Product Reactions

Some dogs are sensitive to certain products like shampoos, conditioners, coat sprays, or flea and/or tick control products. If your dog has an unexplained skin reaction, check if you've recently changed grooming products or food. For dogs with sensitive skin, mild, hypo-allergenic, and/or natural products containing skin-soothing ingredients are good to try. Get a product recommendation from your vet if you are unsure.

Skin Diseases

Dogs can develop many different skin diseases, some inherited, some caused by environmental factors. Your vet should always address skin diseases in your dog and can advise you how to groom around them. Whether relatively minor but inconvenient, such as greasy, scaly skin resulting from overactive sebaceous glands (called oily seborrhea), something cosmetic, like a disease that causes hair loss (like color mutant alopecia), or something potentially life-threatening, like skin cancer, skin disease in dogs must be treated, so please see your vet.

Skin Infections

Skin infections can be caused by bacteria introduced into a wound, by unsanitary conditions, or by poor grooming. From impetigo (common in puppies) to skin-fold pyoderma (common in loose-skinned breeds like Chinese Sharpei) to abscesses of undetermined origin, skin infections should be treated with antibiotics, which your vet can prescribe. Never groom over an infected area. Hair should be cut or carefully clipped from the area so the infection can heal, but let your vet take care of this procedure.

Holistic Skin Care

As holistic health grows in popularity for humans, more and more humans are seeking holistic veterinary care for their pets. From pet massage to acupuncture, therapies abound. Holistic therapies seem to be most effective for chronic health conditions, a category that often includes skin conditions like allergies and dermatitis. Some of the therapies that holistic vets and other holistic animal health care practitioners might recommend for skin problems include acupressure, aromatherapy, herbal therapy, homeopathy, nutritional therapy, and vitamin therapy. Always tell your vet if you are seeking additional care from a holistic source in order to prevent conflicting treatments.

Part 4

There are many natural or hypo-allergenic products available if your dog has sensitive skin.

Sunburn

Dogs can get sunburned, just like people–and they can develop skin cancer, too. You can buy sunscreen for dogs in spray form, especially important for hairless, sparsely coated, and light-colored dogs, and for all light-colored noses. A human sunscreen recommended by your vet can work if your dog won't lick it off, but just to be safe, a non-toxic sunscreen made for dogs is your best choice. Light-colored dogs that will be outside in sunny weather for more than a few minutes should wear sunscreen, and if you take your dog to the beach, re-apply sunscreen just as you would reapply it to yourself.

Natural Products for Gentle Skin Care

Many pet owners whose pets have sensitive skin have searched and searched for products that work but aren't irritating, and many of these people have finally settled on natural products. Natural products tend to be based on natural botanicals rather than chemicals. They use plant extracts that tend to be soothing and healing to the skin. Just because something is called "natural" doesn't mean your dog will necessarily respond well to it. Some dogs have skin reactions to some natural products, but, in general, these products are formulated with sensitive skin in mind.

Some of the ingredients in natural products (shampoos, conditioners, coat sprays, and pest control products) that work with canine skin to keep it healthy and free from irritation include natural oils, aloe vera, menthol and/or eucalyptus oil to combat itching, and garlic (a natural antibiotic). Every company has their own unique formula, so get a veterinary recommendation. You may have to try several products before hitting on one that works well for your pet.

Finally, dogs with sensitive skin will benefit immensely from daily grooming sessions. Constant vigilance to catch skin problems early can make all the difference in how serious a problem becomes.

Down to the Mat

A matted coat is a challenge for any groomer, amateur or professional. Mats are solid masses of hair so knotted they can't be combed out. A matted coat is detrimental to dogs, not only because it looks bad and ruins the coat, but also because it can trap moisture, dirt, and bacteria, compromising the health of your dog's skin, even resulting in sores and infections.

A badly matted dog may have suffered grooming neglect, but the presence of a mat doesn't necessarily indicate a lack of good grooming. True, dogs with long, double, or curly coats can develop mats and consequential skin problems when they aren't kept properly brushed and

A matted coat can test the skills of a groomer.

A mat is a tangle or knot in the hair that resists brushing or combing.

combed, but some breeds develop mats so easily that even with a daily comb-through, a few mats are inevitable here and there, now and then. The trick is to prevent them whenever possible and to know what to do with them when you encounter them.

Dogs should be tangle-free all the way down to the skin, so if you do find a mat or two on your dog, this chapter will help you to get it out and reclaim your dog's healthy, beautiful, snarl-free coat.

The Mechanics of a Mat

A mat is simply a tangle of hair, often with undercoat, that has formed a knot tight enough to resist brushing and combing. Mats tend to form on dogs with thick, long, curly, or double coats in body "corners" and areas with longer hair, such as the base of legs, the anal area under the tail, under the chest by the front legs, and around the ears. In most cases, daily brushing and combing will prevent tangles from turning into mats, but sometimes a mat will surprise you.

Mats form because hair is covered in tiny scales, and when hair is unkempt or harshly treated, those scales can stick up, acting like tiny barbs. These barbs catch shed hairs, wooly undercoat hairs, even dirt and debris, knotting and tangling until they form a solid mass of hair that is virtually impossible to comb through.

Some people tackle mats by cutting them out, which leaves "holes" in the coat, or by shaving the coat all the way off. In severe cases, shaving the coat may be necessary. Regular grooming should preclude this, but if you've let things go (or someone else has and you are grooming their dog), a shave-down-and-start-over approach might be preferable to hours and hours with a mat splitter, scissors, and comb, pulling on the poor dog's coat.

Shed and Mat

Mats sometimes form when a dog is "blowing coat," that approximately annual or bi-annual period when shedding is particularly heavy. A dog dropping big tufts of undercoat that catch in the longer, harder outer coat can form mats in a single day; so can a puppy dropping his juvenile coat and growing in his adult coat.

Part 4

> **Don't Wash That Mat!**
>
> Never wash a matted coat! Water encourages a mat to shrink and tighten, making it much harder to remove. Always remove mats before a bath.

If, however, you have just a few mats and want to save that long and lovely coat, try the techniques explained below for removing a mat.

Tools for Better Mat Removal

The first step in mat removal is to have the right tools. You may be able to get through most mats with a sharp scissors and a comb, but you may also be able to preserve more coat with some specialized equipment and products.

Oil-based coat conditioner spray: Never try to remove a mat without first spraying it with an oil-based coat spray. The oil in this spray smooths down the scales on the hair, essentially taming the "barbs" so that mat comes out more easily. It saturates and loosens the mat.

Mat comb: A mat comb is a kind of comb-like tool with blades instead of teeth used for slicing large mats into small sections that can then be worked out individually.

Mat splitter: A mat splitter is a blade with a curved handle, used to cut through a mat. The curved handle makes the mat splitter easy to hold and easy to slit into the mat.

Sharp scissors: Sometimes, the best way to get through a mat is to cut it into strips. A sharp scissors can do the work of a mat comb or a mat splitter. Always use scissors with extreme care, however, to prevent cutting the dog's skin.

Slicker brush: After cutting the mat into smaller parts, work out the tangles with a slicker brush.

In some cases, a badly matted coat should be shaved down and the hair given a chance to grow back.

After soaking the mat with a conditioning spray, try combing through the hair.

The Price of a Mat

You can spend a lot of money on a lot of different mat-removing tools, which can make mat removal a little easier and faster, or you can make do with a sharp scissors and a comb. You don't have to spend a lot of money to keep your dog mat-free, especially if you prevent mats in the first place by daily brushing and combing.

Steel comb: After cutting through a mat and brushing out the tangles, work through the entire area, down to the skin, working the smaller tangles out with a fine-toothed comb.

How to Remove a Mat, Step By Step

Once you have the right tools in front of you, you can tackle that mat head-on. Here's how.

1. Soak the mat with the oil-based coat conditioner spray. Let the spray penetrate the mat for a few moments, to help loosen it.

2. Starting at the outer edge of the mat, try to pick the mat apart with a comb, pulling a few hairs loose at a time with the comb and your fingers. You can also use the pick-end of a comb (or even a knitting needle) to try to loosen and pull out the mat.

3. If the mat is still too tight and too large to work through with a comb, use a mat comb to saw the mat into several smaller sections.

4. If the mat is smaller, slice through it with a mat splitter.

5. If you decide to use scissors, be very careful. Dog skin isn't attached to the muscle in the same way human skin is, and it can easily tent-up as you pull up hair. It's easy accidentally

Part 4

to cut a dog's skin while trying to cut through a mat. For safety, slide the comb against the skin between the skin and the mat, then cut through the mat over the comb, holding the scissors perpendicular to the comb.

6. Once the mat is cut into smaller pieces, gently brush the pieces out with a slicker brush.

7. Finally, finish with a fine-toothed comb to make sure the entire mat is gone.

8. Follow up by brushing and combing daily.

Keeping some pets mat-free is a real challenge, but remember that your job is to keep your pet healthy, and that includes his skin and coat. If mat removal and constant grooming really aren't for you, you have three choices: Pay a professional groomer, keep your pet clipped short, or choose a short-coated breed. Just don't allow him to suffer from a matted coat and the health problems that could easily ensue. Better to have no coat at all than a coat in a pathetic mass of mats!

Grooming every day will keep the mats away and your dog healthy.

If you do enjoy the brushing long and curly coats require, great! If you find you are pretty good at removing mats, maybe you have hit upon a new career for yourself. The last section of this book will help to get you started if you think you might want to become a professional groomer.

Part 4

Part Five
Getting Started in Professional Grooming

"Can I just send him through? We're on our way to a dog show."

Is Professional Grooming for You?

Maybe you really enjoy grooming your dog. Maybe you think you're pretty good at it. Maybe friends have been asking for your advice about grooming their dogs, or even asking you to do it for them. One person even offered to pay you. Could you have a future as a professional groomer?

Professional pet grooming is an exciting career that offers flexibility, independence, and freedom. Grooming dogs is fun, and it can be lucrative, too. About one-third of grooming business owners make between $30,000 and $40,000 per year, according to PetGroomer.com's 2001 Grooming Industry Survey of 6,493 pet grooming business owners. Another 18 percent reported earning

If you enjoy grooming your dog, this may be the job for you.

Online Resource for Professional Pet Groomers

For a vast and comprehensive resource on professional pet grooming, visit PetGroomer.com. This website seeks to unify professional pet groomers working on their own into a cohesive and communicative whole. From chat boards to grooming contests to everything you ever wanted to know about running a grooming business, this website is a great resource for any professional pet groomer, from beginner to seasoned professional.

between $40,000 and $50,000 from their grooming business, and more than 100,000 people worldwide work as professional pet groomers. Could you become one of them?

However, becoming a professional pet groomer is more than brushing friendly dogs all day. It entails good business planning, patience, people skills, and some pretty rigorous physical labor. This chapter will help you to determine whether you would be willing to accept the kind of life and work necessary for success as a professional pet groomer. Consider each of the questions in terms of your own life, personality, and schedule, to get a sense of whether you just like the *idea* of becoming a dog groomer, or whether the lifestyle of this flexible and interesting career really would appeal to you.

The Good Stuff

You may have already considered many of the wonderful things about being a professional pet groomer. You get to work with dogs. You get to make dogs look beautiful. You even get to make a dog feel better and enjoy better health by maintaining the grooming so crucial to healthy skin, coat, and even movement and vision. Many groomers have been the first to spot lumps, infections, rashes, and other medical problems, and groomers soon learn when to send their clients straight to the veterinarian.

Groomers get to develop relationships with many dogs and get to experience many wonderful dog breeds they couldn't ever own. Those groomers motivated to learn about dogs soon become breed experts, as well as experts in canine health (although good groomers also know when to refer clients to a vet rather than answer crucial health questions on their own).

Self-employed professional groomers get to set their own hours, take on as much or as little work as they like, work at home or in a location of their own choosing, and enjoy the

On the Road

Mobile pet grooming is a fun way to work as a professional groomer. Invest in a good van and you can set up a grooming center that travels all around town, offering grooming in the client's own driveway. Many people love the idea of paying for a grooming "house call" rather than having to drive a dog to and from the groomer, and some pets are much more comfortable staying on the premises for their grooming. Mobile pet grooming is also fun because you get to be outside, visit new places, and travel around all day. The scenery constantly changes, and a day on the road in the grooming van can be full of adventure.

The cost to purchase the van and the necessary portable equipment can be high, but many mobile groomers claim they are back in the black within a year or two in areas where demand for grooming is high. Mobile groomers can usually charge a little more than home or shop groomers for the convenience of the at-home visit. Research grooming needs in your town and see if it might be the perfect place for a mobile groomer—or another mobile groomer, as many towns and cities already have at least one.

freedom and flexibility of owning a business. Mobile pet groomers get to take their show on the road, perfect for people who don't like to be cooped up inside all day.

Even those groomers who are employed at places such as a grooming shop, a pet store, or a veterinarian office often get to set their own hours but may enjoy the additional benefits of group employment: insurance, paid vacation, and bonuses.

Perhaps best of all, the professional pet groomer gets to work with animals every day in a helpful, hands-on, interactive environment. Talk about really getting to know dogs! The professional pet groomer knows more about dogs than most people. If you would like to live this kind of life, professional pet grooming may just be for you.

However, pet grooming certainly isn't easy. Sometime it is hard physical labor. Sometimes it is tedious. Sometimes, it's downright dangerous! ("Nice 145-pound doggy…no need to growl like that…just get into this bathtub and let me hose you down.")

The rest of this chapter contains a series of questions. Consider each question and whether or not it presents something for which you are prepared. It doesn't matter if you've never balanced a checkbook or pacified an irate customer before. What matters is that you are willing to learn. Here's what you should be ready to handle.

Are You Motivated?

One of the reasons many people could never own their own business is motivation. Being your own boss means motivating yourself to get started, get clients, keep the schedule, and clean up. You can hire people, but then you have to supervise and pay them.

Are You a Multi-Tasker?

Operating a business isn't easy, no matter what the business. You have to think about doing the books, scheduling appointments, and dealing with people. You must keep up with changes and innovations in your field, both health-related and tool-related. You must keep your shop clean. All this in addition to grooming dogs! As you brush that Beagle, you might need to be planning how to scissor the Bichon, de-mat the Old English Sheepdog, and make a plan for grooming that moppy mixed-breed before the afternoon is over.

If you aren't good at handling a lot of different tasks at once, you might not enjoy going into business yourself, let alone this business. Another option is to find a business partner who is good at the things you don't want to handle. While you clip the Poodle and bathe the Schnauzer, your partner can balance the books or greet and schedule customers.

Are You a People Person?

Dogs may be your business, but if you are a professional groomer, you also have to deal with people. People are your clients and people pay you, so if you don't know how to be pleasant, friendly, communicative, and open with your clients, you may find you have a hard time operating a successful grooming business. People love their dogs and want their dogs groomed by someone with whom they feel comfortable, so if you make people nervous or they think you aren't friendly, they probably won't want you to groom their dog.

And then there are the people who don't seem to care about their pets at all. You will certainly encounter some people who treat their dogs in a way you won't approve of, from harsh treatment to neglect. As a professional groomer, you can certainly offer advice, suggesting a client seek veterinary care or obedience training. However, in order to stay in business, you must know how to offer advice that can help the dog while remaining politic and non-confrontational to the customer.

Are You a Planner?

Starting a small business takes planning, organization, and decision-making. If you can't plan it, it won't happen, and if you can't keep it organized, it will fall apart. Starting a business takes more than confidence and a good idea. It takes foresight.

Are You Patient?

Many of the above qualities work hand in hand with patience. Dog grooming is not for people who like to rush through things. You have to enjoy doing a thorough (and that sometimes means *slow*) job on the pets you groom. Sometimes grooming is tedious. Sometimes it is downright monotonous. If you can't handle the occasional (and sometimes frequent) day filled with one dog after another with constant bathing and clipping, or if you find you don't have the patience to stand and scissor a Poodle or a Bichon to perfection (in fact, if you don't think it's perfectly fascinating!), you might consider a different career course.

Are You Squeamish?

Dog grooming is more than just clipping, trimming, and brushing. It involves dealing with real live dogs–dogs that aren't yours and who could come to you with medical problems. You might find infections or sores on a dog you are grooming. You might also sometimes encounter a sick or very nervous dog. If the idea of an occasional encounter with dog vomit, diarrhea, or even blood sends you screaming in the opposite direction, this may not be the job for you. If the idea doesn't thrill you but you think you can handle it, you may just have the stomach for dog grooming.

Are You Strong?

Though you probably never considered going into physical training for a career as a dog groomer, grooming takes some strength. You may have to lift a large dog onto a table or coax one out of a

Refusing Service

As a professional pet groomer, you always have the right to refuse service to anyone, or not to groom a dog that represents, in your opinion, an undue risk to you or your employees. Whether a pet owner is rude or a dog seems dangerous, you don't have to take on any client that makes you uncomfortable.

At one point or another, every pet care professional encounters situations in which they believe a pet is at risk or being dangerously mistreated. In such cases, you also have the right to contact the authorities, anonymously if necessary. As a dog professional and an advocate for pets, you may feel it is your responsibility to report abuse.

bathtub. Brushing and combing a large, long-coated dog or clipping a standard Poodle can really tax your arm muscles, and you may spend hours on your feet. If you aren't in good condition, you may find grooming to be very taxing.

Can You Focus?

Pay attention to anything else when scissoring a dog or clipping a delicate area like the edge of an ear or the anal area and you risk seriously injuring someone's beloved pet. Although every groomer can tell a story about an occasional, accidental nick, grooming absolutely requires focus and full attention to the task. You are using sharp tools around living skin, so if you aren't confident that you can learn to use those tools safely and competently, you might consider another career.

Do You Have a Fear of Getting Bitten?

You can get insurance to cover yourself in the case of a dog bite, but you can't get insurance to prevent a dog bite in the first place! Dealing with other people's dogs automatically entails the risk of a dog bite. Even a well-behaved, non-aggressive dog may bite if he feels fearful, cornered, or startled by new surroundings, new people, and strange tools that buzz, hum, and vibrate.

Do You Have Investment Capital?

Even if you open your shop in your own basement, you will need some money to get started. Professional groomers must have high-quality equipment: different types and sizes of brushes, combs, scissors, clippers with blades, blow-dryers, and cages to keep dogs as they wait to be groomed or to be picked up. You should have a grooming table with a harness and a tub for bathing. The higher quality and more ergonomic these crucial pieces of equipment are, the more they cost. You'll also need a variety of products: shampoos, conditioners, coat sprays, tear-stain remover, and flea-control products, not to mention colognes, rubber bands, and a variety of fancy bows and ribbons. And don't forget advertising–that ad in the phone book isn't free.

Eventually, you may even want to include shop rent, decorating expenses, and money to hire and pay employees. All that takes money, so while you can acquire the components for your business a little at a time or all at once, keep in mind that high-quality grooming equipment and supplies aren't cheap. If you don't have the money to spare, you may need to get a small business loan, and then, of course, you have to pay it back (with interest).

Are You Business-Savvy?

Opening a grooming business is about much more than grooming dogs. Running a small business, no matter the business, is complicated and takes a lot of knowledge. You can take classes on running a small business, talk to other local business owners, and do a lot of market research, but when it comes down to opening your business, you'll have to put that knowledge into practice or hire someone you trust to do it for you.

The smaller and less formal a grooming practice you have, the less you will have to deal with the ins and outs of running a business, but if you operate your business for profit (and not just as a hobby), you will need to pay self-employment taxes and file a Schedule C with your income tax form. You'll have to keep track of all your business-related expenses, keep careful books, and operate your business smartly. The more you learn about running a business, the more your grooming operation is likely to prosper, so don't forget that although you may have entered into the profession because you love dogs, you need to know a whole lot about business, too.

Small Business Owners Unite!

Many communities have resources to help new small business owners make smart choices and set up their businesses in ways that will be most likely to succeed. Check your community for small business classes and other resources. Or, search the Internet for information. The website of the US Small Business Administration is an excellent place to start. Full of information and frequently asked questions about starting a small business, this website may just prove invaluable. Check it out at:

http://www.sba.gov/starting/.

What Will Your Family Think?

No matter how excited you get about becoming a professional pet groomer and/or starting your own business, you must consider how it will affect your family. If you plan to begin grooming dogs at home, will your spouse mind having a house full of strangers, not to mention dog hair? Will you mind having dogs around–dogs that could be unpredictable–if you have young children?

Consider also how your income could change. Some people enjoy an increase in income when they become a pet groomer, but others are willing to accept less income for the increased freedom and enjoyment of this career. Is the rest of your family also willing and able to accept a decrease in income? Having your family behind you can make all the difference in whether or not you have the will, motivation, and confidence to succeed.

Are You Willing to Keep Learning?

To be a good groomer is to continue to learn. Styles, techniques, equipment, and products change continually as groomers and manufacturers learn more and as tastes change. The self-employed professional groomer who wants to remain current must make an effort to stay in touch with what is going on in the world of grooming. Attend classes, seminars, and other grooming events. Attend dog shows often and talk to breeders to learn about the latest in grooming different breeds or about how to groom less common breeds. Ask about products, scissoring techniques, the latest shampoo, the best way to use the electric clipper on this breed or that.

Joining a professional organization is a great way to keep current on the grooming market, get business advice, and communicate with other groomers to swap hints, tips, and other helpful information. Consider attending a grooming school where you can learn from the professionals.

Everything you do to learn more about grooming will further your career by adding to your knowledge and experience and by giving your clients confidence that you are growing with the field of professional grooming. Plus, the desire to keep learning will keep your interest in grooming piqued. The more you know, the better you will be, and quality is what keeps your clients coming back.

How to Get Training

Reading this book is an excellent way to begin a career as a professional groomer, but it is only a first step. Dog grooming is a complex and fascinating subject, and dog groomers can continue to learn throughout their careers. You can learn about dog grooming by reading lots of books on the subject, talking to groomers, visiting dog shows, and practicing on your own pets and the pets of willing friends. If you are motivated, you can learn quite a bit on your own and can even make a good career for yourself as a professional groomer simply from experience you gain "in the field."

However, many pet groomers decide to get professional training, often after doing some

Training is an important part of becoming a groomer.

Grooming Career Stats

According to PetGroomer.com's most recent survey of career seekers in the pet grooming industry:

- 67 percent planned to be self-employed, while 23 percent were seeking employment by an already-established grooming operation.

- 63 percent expected to start their grooming careers employed by an already-established grooming operation.

- 85 percent of pet grooming business owners were employed by someone else as a pet groomer before they became a business owner.

- 66 percent have never worked with pets before.

- 81 percent are female.

- 77 percent plan to become certified by a pet-grooming organization.

- 81 percent plan to learn dog grooming for pets, while only 12 percent plan to learn professional grooming for show dogs. (29 percent also plan to learn how to groom cats.)

reading and research on their own. According to PetGroomer.com, 81 percent of those surveyed who were seeking a career in pet grooming were planning on attending a school of pet grooming.

Whether you choose to go it alone or attend a professional school, you can get training from a variety of sources, and sometimes the best and most thorough way is to use as many of them as you can. Here's how to navigate the options.

Grooming School

Pet grooming schools are popping up all over the country as more and more people express interest in entering this fun profession. Attending a grooming school can give your grooming career a great boost. Many schools teach hands-on grooming of many different breeds, include hundreds of hours of informative courses, and even offer courses on starting and managing your own business. Some schools offer certification, diplomas, and other credits that you can display and use in your advertising after you graduate.

However, not all pet grooming schools are the same or offer the same kinds of classes and credits. Some are geared for more modest career goals like bathing and prep, while others offer more ambitious educational programs, launching you into a truly professional career as a highly skilled groomer. Therefore, don't assume that the pet grooming school nearest you is just as good as the one in a different part of the country or is geared toward the goals you have set up for yourself.

Pet groomers often express frustration that more schools don't exist. Sure, it's easier to travel less than an hour to get to school, but the advantages for your future career and income could well depend on which school you choose. If traveling farther means you'll end up with a better career, you may decide such an effort and expense is worth it.

> ### How They Learned
>
> According to the 2001 Grooming Business Owner Survey conducted by PetGroomer.com, 42 percent of grooming business owners attended a pet grooming school; 48 percent apprenticed under a pet groomer; and 10 percent learned from a correspondence or video course or were self-taught.

But how do you know if a grooming school is worth the price in tuition? Or if grooming school is for you at all? Let's look at that second question first.

Do I Really Want to Go to School?

If you are already pretty sure you want to become a professional pet groomer, you may have many of the qualities a successful pet grooming school student requires: patience, a love of animals, a desire to become a good groomer, and the wish to have a job that offers freedom and flexibility.

However, going to a grooming school also requires some other qualities. Consider the following questions.

• Can you take constructive criticism and learn from it rather than be offended by it? Grooming school teachers are there to help you improve, but you have to be willing to learn from them.

• Do you enjoy learning in a more structured environment, or do you prefer figuring out things on your own?

• Are you willing to learn about business as well as grooming? Are you interested in starting your own grooming shop or getting a job in a shop owned by someone else? Your preference could determine what kind of school you should attend.

• Can you afford the tuition? Are you willing to take out a student loan? Many schools have loan programs, but not all of them do.

• Can you afford the time to take the classes–time that you can't spend working at another job or spending with your family–in order to further your education?

• Have you graduated from high school or the equivalent? Some schools require this.

> ## Are You Licensed?
>
> Currently, no state requires pet groomers to be formally licensed, but many groomers are lobbying to have licensure enacted, in order to ensure quality control and to give the profession greater credibility. Grooming *schools,* however, should be licensed.

If grooming school still sounds like a pretty good idea to you, start looking at schools. Here's how.

Finding the Right Grooming School

Good grooming schools aren't available in every state, but even if you live down the road from a grooming school, that doesn't mean it is the *right* grooming school. Look around the country at different schools. Ask for their catalogues, look at their websites if they have them, and visit them if you can. Read over the information on each school carefully. Look for signs that the school is reputable, offers quality instruction by experienced professionals, and has a program that will teach you what you need to know. Here are some questions to consider.

• Is the school state licensed? Is the school accredited?

• How long has the school been in business? What is their reputation? (Ask professional groomers if they have heard of the school.)

• Who are the teachers? What are their credentials? Are the classes actually taught by the teachers advertised in the school materials, or are some classes taught by assistants?

• What are all the costs associated with attending the school, from tuition, books, and equipment to food, lodging, and travel?

• How many hours of instruction are available? Many schools offer basic courses, advanced courses, and professional courses, but compare the hours offered at various schools, which can vary by quite a lot, from 200 to 900 hours of coursework and training for professional-level tracks. Obviously, programs that offer more hours take longer to complete and are usually more extensive, although some shorter-hour tracks are extra intensive. Many of these hours may be "lab" hours of hands-on dog grooming, complemented by lecture hours of classroom learning. Generally, more hours means you'll come out with more experience.

• What diplomas, certifications, or other credentials does the school award or make available to graduates? How will these credentials translate to the state where you plan to work, if the school is in a different state?

Groomer on Campus

Visit any schools you are seriously considering attending *before* registering for their program and paying tuition. What if the school itself isn't anything like what it says on the website or in the brochure? A school can look and feel much different in person—some may be less professional than they would have you think, and others may be even more impressive. Ask for a tour of the facility and a personal interview with the director so you can get a feel for whether or not your tuition money and time will be well spent.

• What percentage of graduates is currently employed as groomers? Does the school keep other records of graduate successes?

Asking questions, doing your research, and extensively comparing different grooming schools is the best way to figure out which school offers the program and quality you seek. Maybe the school down the road is indeed the perfect school for you, but only after doing your research can you be sure. The more you know about different schools, the more you will have a sense of what makes you comfortable and confident.

When you've finally decided on a school, congratulations! You have some exciting learning to do, and gaining credentials via professional training will give you more information as well as more confidence and experience so that you can best succeed in your new career.

What About Grooming Correspondence Courses?

Many opportunities exist to learn dog grooming via correspondence course. These courses are less expensive and take less time than attending a grooming school. But can you learn how to groom dogs via correspondence? Well, that depends.

Correspondence courses take lots of extra motivation on the part of the student. You have to study the material and watch the demonstration videos without any teacher standing over you or any fellow students to encourage you. You don't gain the same sense of community you do from a grooming school. You also don't have real dogs to practice on or teachers present to help correct your technique, explain things you don't understand, or guide you in the right direction.

On the other hand, if attending a grooming school isn't an option for you, either due to time or financial constraints, a grooming correspondence course could be just what you need to get you started. If you are willing to get out there and supplement your grooming course with lots of hands-on practice, such as through an apprenticeship with a local professional groomer, you may find this kind of learning experience invaluable.

Correspondence courses are all different, but look for one that gives both grooming information and information on running a small business. The course should also have detailed information on how to groom many different breeds. Compare the cost of the course with grooming schools to get a perspective on whether the price is right, and if possible, get recommendations about the course from others.

Staying Current

Though most grooming schools are primarily designed to teach amateur groomers and others with little to no knowledge about pet grooming how to become professionals, many schools also offer courses to keep established and seasoned groomers up-to-date on the most current trends, tools, and techniques. Even after you have secured employment, don't neglect these opportunities for continuing education.

Finally, stay motivated to get your money's worth. If you work through all the material, you'll probably gain quite a bit of valuable knowledge.

Networking

Whether or not you go to grooming school, networking is extremely important for the grooming professional. Groomers have traditionally been unorganized as a profession, existing in pockets around the country without much communication—until recently. Now that pet grooming is becoming such a popular career, pet groomers are getting organized, with some great results.

One of the primary ways groomers have organized

themselves is through professional associations. These associations put on events, share information, and otherwise unite the profession in many productive ways. Some lobby for licensing requirements for groomers (not currently a requirement, but available in some states), some conduct meetings or trade shows, and all provide their members with valuable and continually updated relevant information for professional groomers.

Many grooming associations exist on the state level, and a few are national and/or international. Look up grooming associations in your state at the PetGroomer.com website page for grooming associations or begin by looking into the currently active national grooming associations. Look in the Resources section of this book for contact information on these grooming associations and more.

Be a Self-Starter

Finally, the best groomers are self-starters—those rare individuals who get out there and learn without anyone telling them to do it. If grooming truly interests you, you can play a significant part in your own training. The world is filled with great information for groomers. All you have to do is go out and find it. Here are some ideas.

• Read every grooming book you can get your hands on. You'll soon see that some are more informative than others, some are more specialized or more general than others, and some are aimed more at pet owners. Read them all!

• Continually check the Internet for updated grooming information. Visit PetGroomer.com often, as this site contains links to thousands of grooming-related web pages and is constantly updated. Look around at the personal websites of other groomers, too, to get ideas and information.

• Talk to other groomers at every possible opportunity, whether informally or by getting involved with groups like those listed above.

• Commit to continuing education. Attend conferences, educational seminars, and other training sessions.

• Subscribe to pet grooming trade magazines such as *Groom & Board* and *Groomer to Groomer*, as well as pet industry trade magazines that contain grooming sections, such as

Know Your Dogs

In addition to subscribing to grooming and other pet industry publications, pet groomers can benefit from keeping up with general dog magazines that focus on purebred dogs, many of which cover current grooming information. Take a look at *Dog Fancy, AKC Gazette, Dog World, and Off Lead* magazines. You can learn more than grooming from these magazines. You can learn about the structure, temperaments, strengths, faults, and relevant issues (from legal issues to health issues) of different purebred dogs, and of dogs in general. This kind of information can help you keep your finger on the pulse of the dog-owning public, and it can help you better relate to your customers and care for their pets.

Pet Product News, Pet Business, and *Pet Age.*

• Visit dog shows to teach yourself about all the different breeds. Hang around the benching area and talk to the groomers as they do their work to learn the latest on grooming show dogs. Ask about equipment, products, and the best way to achieve show ring style. (Please be aware when a dog is about to enter a ring, it isn't the best time to grill the handler about grooming!)

• Also continue to learn about small business practices if you own your business, even if you operate it from your basement. Take small business seminars and read up on small business operations. Check into local or state laws related to grooming and housing animals.

Taking an interest in your own grooming career is the most important thing you can do to further your own training. Get excited about the finer points of both grooming and running a business and you'll motivated yourself to learn more and more. Soon you'll have a name for yourself, a sound professional reputation, and lo and behold, you're a professional groomer!

How to Set Up Your Business

You're trained, you've practiced, you're ready to go! Or are you? Setting up your own business and joining the ranks of the self-employed may sound glamorous, but it takes a lot of planning, preparation, and (you guessed it) money! Maybe you have a small stash put away to help launch your in-home business, or maybe you plan to get a bank loan, rent a shop, and buy all-new, state-of-the-art equipment. Both routes take planning and some serious considerations about how you will set up, operate, and, eventually, grow your business.

Although setting up your business will be more or less complex depending on what kind of business you are planning–grooming the pets of friends in

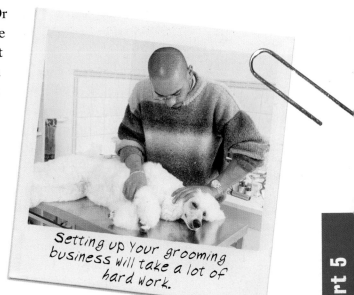

Setting up your grooming business will take a lot of hard work.

your garage or basement is much less of an undertaking than opening up your own shop in a separate retail space—any self-employment will be more profitable, not to mention more enjoyable, if you have a plan and cover all your bases. This chapter will help you to consider some of the things involved in setting up your own pet grooming business.

Writing a Business Plan

A business plan is essential for anybody planning to take out a business loan. A bank may or may not want to see one, but when you have a large financial stake in a business, a business plan is invaluable in helping you to clarify your goals, organize your finances, and set up long-term goals for growing your business. Plus, a business plan helps you to put all your goals, needs, and other considerations down on paper.

But what about the home groomer who wants to start that part-time operation in the basement through word-of-mouth? A business plan makes sense for you, too, for all the same reasons. You also need to plan. What will you charge people? How much will equipment cost? Have you thought about how many clients you can handle, and how much money you plan to make?

A business plan puts your goals into perspective, from small to large. Include everything from a specific list of what equipment you will need to a ten-year income/expense forecast. Everything you do once you launch your business will go more smoothly if you've thought about it beforehand and written down a plan.

Many resources exist to help you write a business plan. Most towns and cities have at least one small business resource center, often a branch of the government's Small Business Administration. These centers are definitely worth a visit for the resources and help (often free!) that they provide. No matter how small or informal your grooming business, you will undoubtedly get some sound and helpful information. Besides, who knows how you may decide to expand your business later. Those who think ahead are less likely to encounter unfortunate surprises.

The Internet and the library are other good resources for small business information of all kinds, including business plan writing. You should be able to find lots of sample business plans to give you an idea of format and content. Read over examples of business plans so you get a feel for what to include. You can also buy software that will help you to write a good business plan.

As you educate yourself about becoming self-employed (even if it is only on the side, in addition to your "regular" job), you can expand and tweak your business plan. Type your business plan into a computer and print it out. Proofread to be sure your business plan is correct and professional-looking. Then, if you do decide to take the leap and get a small business loan, you'll be ready.

Your business plan can take any form you want, but it should probably include the following information. Title each section separately, as appropriate for your particular goals:

Summary Statement

This section sets out your overall purpose. In a few pages, describe exactly what your business will be. Who is involved, what will you do, where will you do it, and how many clients do you envision having? Keep this part succinct and informational, summarizing but not going into detail about where you will groom, what services you will offer, how much money you will need to get started, etc.

Growth Plan

In this section, set up a schedule. Begin with where you are right now in terms of getting started. Then, describe your goal for this year, next year, five years, and ten years down the line. Be specific in your goals for clients, space, equipment, and income. Sure, you don't know how things will turn out, but if you have goals, you will have a better chance of shaping your business into exactly what you want, within a realistic time frame.

All About You

In this section, detail your own experience, training, and other qualifications. Did you attend grooming school? Did you apprentice under someone? Are you just getting started in your plan? Write about how you know what you know, or be specific about your plans for furthering your knowledge and experience in the field of grooming. If you will have a

Your Grooming Equipment Wish List

Maybe you dream of a vacuum attachment for your clipper, to conveniently suck away unwanted hair, but for now you know you'll have to make due with a regular clipper and a broom. Maybe you wish for a hydraulic tub but, for now, you will have to lift those big dogs as well as you can. Yet, you know you will invest in the best possible set of professional scissors, a spacious grooming table, and an industrial-strength cage dryer.

Whatever your priorities, make a detailed list of the equipment you know you will need right away, and an additional grooming equipment "wish list" of products you plan to attain eventually. Having these items on paper and planning ahead for when you would like to purchase them will help you when you see a real deal on a hydraulic tub or a vacuum attachment for those clippers. You can follow, or adjust, your financial plan accordingly, knowing that you aren't making purchases on a whim.

business partner or employees, give each person a separate paragraph and discuss that individual's qualifications: knowledge, experience, training, and/or plans for further training.

What Will You Offer?

In this section, explain in detail exactly what your business will provide to clients. Will you be a bathing operation only? A full-service groomer for pets? In detail, list the specific services you plan to provide, and how much you plan to charge for them. What will you do, and what won't you do? Decide what your hours will be, or whether you will groom by appointment only. Will you have a shop front with parking or a separate entrance to your home? How far ahead can people schedule appointments?

Also discuss what equipment and products you will use on pets. Will you make those products for sale, or will you be strictly a service operation and not a retail store? Also decide what extras you will offer. Training? Veterinary referrals? A free grooming with every ten, or other incentives for regular clients? Remember, you can always add to this section as you learn more.

Who Are Your Clients?

In this section, discuss who you envision your client base to be. Will you have a high-end boutique-style shop for fancy cuts and show dogs? Or maybe you will cater to the hunting dogs in your rural area, or the pampered toy dogs in the neighboring high-rise apartments. Be specific about whom you plan to serve. If you live in a small town, perhaps you will offer all-purpose grooming to the general population. Or, if you plan to cater to a niche market, explain that here.

This is also the section to report a little research. How many other groomers work in your area? Are there mobile groomers? In-home groomers? Grooming shops? Where are they located compared to your shop? Also, if possible, compile statistics about how many pets live in your area, to determine whether you will fill a need. If you are trying to get a loan from a bank, they will want to know your shop isn't superfluous, and that you will actually be able to attract customers.

Advertising

Speaking of attracting customers, how will people know about you? Do you plan to take out an ad in the local paper? Invest in a Yellow Pages listing? Install a sign outside your shop? Design a logo and include it on everything—your sign, your business cards, your stationary, your invoices. Consider, in detail, your plans for marketing your business, small or large. You might be the best groomer for a hundred miles around, but if nobody knows about you, your skills won't do anybody any good.

The Bottom Line

Finally, it's time to talk money. How much money do you have, how much will you need to get started, and how much do you plan to make? What will you charge for various services? What are your estimated operating expenses? If you plan to borrow money, what will you use it for? Break that down in detail.

If you are planning on getting a loan, you can also include your own financial information here: how much you make, how much you owe, your credit history, etc.

Planning Your Space

A business plan is only as good as your own planning about what exactly you will need to set up shop, and that includes looking closely at some of the bare bones of running your own business. A grooming shop in particular necessitates some very specific requirements for space. You must have enough room, enough electrical power, a convenient source of water, and sufficient lighting. You should have a customer waiting area, a separate bathing and drying area, and a separate clipping/trimming area.

It's much better to find a space in the beginning that works, that will meet a growing need for electricity and water, that is easy to clean and sanitize (for instance, tiled instead of carpeted), and that has enough room to move around without bumping into walls or other employees. Also, be sure the space you are considering is properly zoned and that you are aware of all the necessary local codes and other regulations that would apply to a business with heavy electrical and water use and that permits animals. What will happen if dogs soil on the sidewalk or urinate on the building? What will happen if barking bothers neighboring tenants? Look into all the options *before* signing a lease!

If you plan to groom at home, you will probably need to have a dedicated space. Is the basement light enough? Is the garage warm enough? Is the garden shed large enough? Are you prepared for the increase in water and electricity? And can you install a tub, set up a grooming table, put in drying cages, and keep the area sufficiently cool when blow-dryers are running in July?

Up to Code?

Certain local codes and other regulations may also apply to home groomers. Not all residential areas are the same when it comes to home businesses. Your area may have restrictions applying to traffic (your clients have to park somewhere), animals, pet waste, noise, and utility usage. If the neighbors complain about dogs coming and going all day long, will you know where you stand, legally? What if clients don't clean up after their pets? How much water will you actually use when bathing pets all day? Consider all the possibilities so you aren't caught off guard by a citation, an eviction notice, or even a lawsuit.

Don't Forget the IRS

As someone who is self-employed, remember that you will also have to pay taxes. No one will be withholding federal income tax from your paycheck if you are your own boss. That means you have to pay taxes yourself. You can hire someone to figure out your tax situation or you can do it on your own, but in most cases, you will need to pay quarterly taxes (pre-paying your amount due in April), which will include a special self-employment tax made just for those of us who work for ourselves. This can add up, so don't forget to include those quarterly tax payments in your budget.

Growing Your Business

Even if you are merely daydreaming about opening a grooming business today, consider that if you do start grooming from home, your grooming business may well grow. Groomers are in high demand! How would you handle a burgeoning business? Would you plan to put a limit on clients, or would you prefer to expand and even hire employees eventually?

If the latter, consider how you might be able to add on to your home or otherwise expand to meet future needs. Could you add on to the garage, or put a grooming shop addition onto your house?

It's exciting to think about your future as an independent business owner, a pet groomer setting your own hours and working with animals. Just remember that any successful business takes a lot of work, dedication, self-discipline, and especially careful planning.

Safety and Liability Issues

Running your own pet grooming business can be profitable, fun, and satisfying. However, like any other business, it has risks that come with the rewards. Many aspects of pet grooming can quickly turn into safety and/or liability issues, but the pet groomer that is prepared for these issues will handle them, should they arise, in the best possible way.

This chapter isn't meant to be a comprehensive discussion of every single thing that could possibly go wrong with your business. Instead, consider it a place to start building your awareness of your responsibility both as a small business owner and the temporary caretaker of animals cherished by others.

Be prepared for any situation in your grooming business.

This chapter is also not meant to be a source of legal advice. I am not a lawyer and cannot advise you on legal issues! Instead, this chapter is intended to alert you to some of the many safety, liability, and legal issues that could, potentially, arise for a pet groomer. Should you find yourself in a situation in which you require legal counsel, please seek a qualified professional.

Put It in Writing

Something about a visual helps everybody understand things better. When you first start grooming, you may be tempted to ask people what they think is a "fair" price, or you may be tempted to give friends a different, lower price. Even when they don't mean to, however, people will take advantage of this kind of "casual" service. If you act like a professional from the beginning, most people wouldn't consider or expect a special deal.

Post your services and the cost of each so they are clearly visible, either in a brochure or on a sign (or both). If people can look and see exactly how much a bath costs or how much different clips are, they won't argue. When people know exactly what to expect, they are more likely to be satisfied with the result.

Also, pictures of different clips on the walls make it easy for pet owners to point and say, "I want that." (Be sure you post only those clips you know how to do!) Describe your services so people can see what, exactly, they are getting for their money, and don't be afraid to describe special high-end equipment or products you use. List choices of products and prices of each–say, a basic shampoo may be one price, but a special whitening or darkening shampoo a slightly higher price. Will you charge more for a hand-scissoring than a quick all-over clip? State that on your price list, and describe the difference.

Printing brochures isn't nearly the complicated and expensive job it once was. All you need is a personal computer and a printer. Design a brochure yourself using one of many user-friendly software programs. If you don't want to invest in a fancy price board for your store, consider a dry-erase board or chalkboard, easy to revise and update.

In other words, let customers read for themselves exactly what you can provide for them and how much it will cost. If anything should happen such that a customer is dissatisfied, you'll be in a more solid position to defend yourself if you can point to the brochure and say, "This is what you asked for, and this is what I did."

Safety First!

You work with water, slippery floors, and electronic equipment. You also work with animals that possess sharp teeth and claws. Put them all together and you have the potential for accidents! Even if you don't hire employees, you should take every precaution to keep yourself from getting injured. If you get hurt, you can't do your job (and those small business loan payments aren't going to make themselves).

Every shop and in-home grooming business is different. Designing a safe workplace depends on the design of your shop, your equipment choices, and, to a large extent, how well you keep things cleaned up, maintained, and operating correctly.

Whose Dog Is This?

Every groomer should have a system to ensure that dogs are returned to their proper owners. Although you may not believe you could make such a mistake, two dogs of the same breed can look a lot alike. Maybe you will write up a ticket for each dog as it comes in and keep that ticket with that dog throughout the entire grooming process. Maybe you will have a color-coded system. Whatever your system, have one.

Keeping your work environment safe requires a little planning and a lot of maintenance. To create and maintain a safe workplace, follow (or adapt, as appropriate) the following, adding any others that are relevant to your unique situation.

Structural Safety

• Be sure you have enough electrical outlets to handle your electricity load.

• Put filters in drains to catch pet hair to help prevent plumbing problems.

• Carry insurance on your house/shop to cover fire, weather damage, theft, vandalism, etc.

Your Safety

• Always mop any water off the floor immediately–don't wait! If you can't do it, delegate the task right away.

• Apply non-skid surfaces to floors in heavy-traffic areas, such as rubber matting that is easy to pull up and hose off if necessary.

• Sit whenever possible. You'll be on your feet enough!

• Use tools that feel comfortable. Professional tools tend to be more ergonomic and easier on your hands.

• Keep scissors and blades sharp for ease of use.

• Invest in the quietest possible equipment to preserve your own hearing and for the least possible stress (pet grooming gets loud enough!).

• Remember that grooming products, especially those containing pest control chemicals, can cause skin reactions. Wear gloves to protect your skin.

• Wear eye protection.

• Attend pet trade shows to keep abreast of the latest in safe and ergonomic equipment and products.

Pet Safety

• Always examine pets before you groom them. If a pet appears sick or injured in any way, don't groom the pet. Instead, alert the owner. Have a clearly stated policy in your brochure or on a sign that states you will not groom sick or injured pets. Calling attention to any problems before you groom can help the owner to seek veterinary attention for the pet. It will also keep you from getting blamed for a pre-existing condition.

What Are You, a Doctor?

You may not be a doctor, but you should seriously consider including malpractice insurance in your business policy. If you accidentally injure someone's pet, you could face a huge lawsuit. Better safe than sorry.

• Avoid electrocution risk—never bathe pets near electrical appliances/tools, and be sure your clipping station isn't right next to the bathing station.

• Pay attention to your work while clipping and scissoring! Don't watch television, listen to music, or chit-chat, risking pet injury.

• Change clipper blades often so they don't overheat and burn pets.

• Use non-skid surfaces in tubs and on grooming tables.

• Always secure pets in tubs and on grooming tables with collar/leash assemblies.

• Be prepared for the possibility of dog fights–not all dogs get along and all pets must be secured to prevent disaster.

• Don't put it past that wet dog to leap out of the tub and out the front door. Always secure uncaged pets. A double door–one leading to a foyer, a second leading to the outside–can also help foil a runaway.

Your Liability

But what if, despite your best efforts, something does go wrong? Are you liable? Chances are, you could be. Any business that involves clients and their beloved pets, not to mention equipment use, has the potential for liability, and any small business owner should be aware of liability issues.

Every professional pet groomer should have 1) an attorney, and 2) adequate insurance coverage. From paperwork issues to lawsuits, an attorney can help you handle any legal issues appropriately and with minimum risk to you.

Do you need a business license? Should you be a sole proprietorship or a corporation? Your attorney can help you with these questions. Should you sign that lease? Buy that policy? Do you apologize to the pet owner who unleashed her own dog on your property and her dog was struck by a car? And what about that complaint from your neighbor about barking dogs, or that lawsuit your client is threatening because you accidentally nicked her show dog with a scissors? Don't answer that–ask your attorney first!

Owning your own business is a complicated, well...business! A professional legal advisor isn't a luxury but a necessity.

Do-It-Yourself Taxes?

Depending on your motivation, time, and confidence, you may be able to do your own taxes with tax software designed for the small business owner. For some, however, an accountant is well worth the price, to help ensure your small business return is prepared correctly. However, don't depend on your accountant to come up with every possible deduction. That's up to you. Save your receipts and keep careful track of your categorized income and expenses like equipment, products, rent, and utilities. Even if you groom from home, you should be able to deduct a portion of your home expenses as business expenses.

Whether you've launched a burgeoning local retail establishment or are perfectly content to groom the pets of a few friends in your basement, make safety a priority. If that means grooming a little bit slower or spending a little more on equipment, clean-up, electrical work, and plumbing, remember that your extra time and care will only enhance your reputation as a safe, responsible, caring professional.

Remember that you went into this business because you love dogs and want to work with them and help them to be healthier and more beautiful. That's great! But that also means paying attention, being careful, using the best possible equipment, not taking on more than you can handle, taking responsibility for your actions and your work, and finally, protecting both your clients and yourself with clear policies, good insurance coverage, legal backup, and your very best work. What more could a pet owner want from a groomer?

And, as your clients become more loyal, as your client base grows, and as your shop expands, you'll wonder how you could have ever tolerated any other job. You are a pet groomer, and you are great at your job because you never stop learning, growing, and improving.

Congratulations on the achievement of your career goal!

photo Gallery

Smooth-Coated Breeds

American Foxhound

American Staffordshire Terrier

Basenji

Basset Hound

Beagle

Black and Tan Coonhound

Bloodhound

Boston Terrier

Boxer

Bulldog

Bullmastiff

Bull Terrier

Chihuahua (smooth)

Chinese Sharpei

Chinese Crested (smooth)

Dalmatian

Dachshund (smooth)

Doberman Pinscher

English Foxhound

Smooth Fox Terrier

French Bulldog

German Shorthaired Pointer

Great Dane

Greater Swiss Mountain Dog

Greyhound

Harrier

Ibizan Hound

Italian Greyhound

Labrador Retriever

Manchester Terrier

Mastiff

Pointer

Pharaoh Hound

Pug

Rhodesian Ridgeback

Rottweiler

Staffordshire Bull Terrier

Viszla

Weimaraner

Whippet

Medium-Coated Breeds

Akita

Alaskan Malamute

American Eskimo Dog

Australian Cattle Dog

Australian Shepherd

Belgian Malinois

Belgian Sheepdog

Belgian Tervuren

Bernese Mountain Dog

Borzoi

Border Collie

Brittany

Cardigan Welsh Corgi

Chesapeake Bay Retriever

Clumber Spaniel

Collie (smooth)

English Springer Spaniel

Field Spaniel

Finnish Spitz

Flat-Coated Retriever

German Shepherd Dog

Golden Retriever

Great Pyrenees

Kuvasz

Norwegian Elkhound

Pembroke Welsh Corgi

Saint Bernard

Saluki

Schipperke

Siberian Husky

Shiba Inu

Sussex Spaniel

Tibetan Spaniel

Welsh Springer Spaniel

Long-Coated Breeds

Afghan Hound

Bearded Collie

Briard

Chihuahua (longhaired)

Cocker Spaniel

Chow Chow

Collie (rough)

Dachshund (longhaired)

English Cocker Spaniel

English Setter

English Toy Spaniel

Gordon Setter

Havanese

Irish Setter

Japanese Chin

Keeshond

Lhasa Apso

Maltese

Newfoundland

Old English Sheepdog

Papillion

Pekingese

Pomeranian

Samoyed

Shetland Sheepdog

Shih Tzu

Silky Terrier

Skye Terrier

Tibetan Terrier

Yorkshire Terrier

Wirehaired/Broken-Coated Breeds

Affenpinscher

Airedale Terrier

Australian Terrier

Border Terrier

Bouvier des Flandres

Brussels Griffon

Cairn Terrier

Dandie Dinmont Terrier

Wire Fox Terrier

German Wirehaired Pointer

Giant Schnauzer

Miniature Schnauzer

Standard Schnauzer

Irish Terrier

Irish Wolfhound

Lakeland Terrier

Norfolk Terrier

Norwich Terrier

Otterhound

Petit Basset Griffon Vendeen

Scottish Deerhound

Scottish Terrier

Sealyham Terrier

Soft Coated Wheaten Terrier

West Highland White Terrier

Wirehaired Pointing Griffon

Curly-Coated Breeds

American Water Spaniel

Bedlington Terrier

Bichon Frise

Curly-Coated Retriever

Irish Water Spaniel

Kerry Blue Terrier

Komondor

Miniature Poodle

Portuguese Water Dog

Puli

Glossary

Angulation

The angles formed by the different joints in the skeleton.

Apple head

A rounded, domed skull, such as that in the Chihuahua.

Bat ear

An erect, broad-at-the-base ear, such as in the French Bulldog.

Beard

The thick, long hair on the underjaw, such as on a Schnauzer.

Bitch

A female canine (the technical term for a male canine is "dog").

Bite

The position of the upper and lower teeth when the jaws are closed.

Blaze

A white stripe running down the center of the face, often between the eyes.

Bloom

The sheen of a healthy coat.

Blue

A coat color resulting in a genetically diluted black coat.

Bracelets

The rounded tufts of hair on the back legs of the Poodle in a Continental clip or English Saddle clip.

Brachycephalic

The condition of having a flat face, short nose, and elongated soft palate, sometimes resulting in respiratory problems and always resulting in a low heat tolerance.

Breed standard

The official written description of how a particular breed should look.

Brindle

A coat pattern characterized by layered black with a lighter color, resembling a tiger stripe.

Broken-haired

A harsh, wiry coat; also called wire-haired.

Brows

The bony ridges above the eyes, left covered in tufted hair in some breeds.

Brush tail

A bushy or heavily coated tail.

Burr

The inside of the ear.

Button ear

An ear that folds forward with the tip lying close to the skull to cover the ear opening.

Canines

The two upper and two lower larger, pointed teeth between the incisors and the premolars.

Cape

The thick, more heavily coated area of coat over the shoulders, occurring in many breeds.

Carpals

Wrist bones.

Cat foot

A round, compact food with arched, tight toes.

Clip

The particular cut or trim of the coat in breeds whose coat allows for different styles, such as a Poodle, Bichon, or Schnauzer.

Clipped/Shaved Bands

The shaved areas between bracelets on the back legs of a Poodle.

Coat

The hair that covers a dog's skin, either single or in many breeds, a double coat with an outer and undercoat.

Condition

How a dog looks overall, including coat, skin, muscle tone, and behavior.

Conformation

The physical attributes of the dog; the shape, structure, outline, etc., as described in the official written breed standard for that breed.

Crescents

Curved clipped areas on the flanks of a Poodle in the English Saddle clip.

Cropping

The cutting of the ear leather to make the ears stand up or have a particular appearance.

Culotte

The long hair on the backs of the legs of some breeds.

Dapple

A mottled coat pattern of dark patterns over light, characteristic of some breeds such as Dachshunds.

Dentition

The quality of having 42 adult teeth.

Dewclaw

The vestigial "toe" on the inside of the leg. Pet owners and breeders sometimes have the dewclaws surgically removed by a veterinarian.

Dewlap

The loose, hanging skin on the throat of some breeds.

Docking

The cutting of a tail after birth to shorten it.

Dog

A term used by breeders to refer to male dogs (as opposed to "bitch" for female dogs).

Double coat

A common type of coat in many breeds, in which the outer coat is harsher and weather-resistant, while the undercoat is softer and downier for warmth.

Drop ears

Ears that drop down to the sides or are otherwise folded over.

Entropion

A genetic condition causing the eyelid to turn in toward the eyeball. This can cause eye irritation and even corneal abrasion as the eyelashes hit the cornea.

Erect ears

Ears that stand straight up or point out at an angle. Also called "prick ears."

Fall

Hair that hangs over the face, an appropriate style in some breeds.

Feathering

Wispy feathers of hair in a coat.

Flag tail

A long fringed tail carried high like a flag.

Fluffies

A long, overly feathered coat, considered a fault in the show ring.

Fringes

Feathering.

Furnishings

Long hair on the extremities of some breeds; head, tail, legs.

Gazehound

Another word for "sighthound."

Hackles

The part of the coat on the back and neck that raises when the dog is afraid or on the alert.

Hare foot

A type of foot in which the two middle "toes" are noticeably longer than the outer and inner toe; this kind of foot appears relatively long, like a rabbit's foot.

Harlequin

A coat pattern of black or grey patches over white.

Herding dogs

Any of the breeds that herd cattle, sheep, or even waterfowl; as pets, these breeds may herd cats, children, or other dogs. Examples include Border Collies, Old English Sheepdogs, German Shepherds, and Pulis.

Hound

A dog used to hunt by sight or scent.

Hound-marked

The bi-colored or tri-colored coat pattern common to many hound breeds (and some other breeds), characterized by a white background with tan and/or black marks on the head, black, legs, and tail. The exact location of marks varies by breed and individual.

Isabella

A fawn color characteristic of some breeds such as Dobermans and Dachshunds.

Leather

The ear flap.

Liver

A deep reddish brown coat color.

Mane

The long thick hair over the neck, characteristic of some breeds such as Chows and Pomeranians.

Marcel coat

Continuous waves, as in some American Water Spaniels.

Merle

A mottled coat pattern of dark streaks over light characteristic of some breeds such as Collies.

Mottled

A coat pattern of dark round marks on a lighter background, as with the Australian Cattle Dog.

Non-sporting dogs

An American Kennel Club group of breeds that don't fit into other categories such as Sporting, Toy, or Working. Examples include the Chow Chow, Dalmatian, Lhasa Apso, Bichon Frise, and Chinese Sharpei.

Parti-colored

A coat pattern of two or more mottled colors occurring in patches; also called pied or piebald.

Pastern

The front leg between the wrist and toes.

Pedigree

The written record of a dog's ancestry, tracing back relatives for at least three generations.

Peppering

White and black hairs mixed together.

Pied

Large patches of at least two colors. Also called piebald or parti-colored.

Prick ears

Ears that stand straight up or point out at an angle. Also called "erect ears."

Roan

Colored and white hairs finely intermingled.

Ruff

The longer, thick haircoat around the neck, shoulders, and chest of some breeds; the mane.

Sable

A coat of black-tipped hairs on a background of silver, grey, fawn, or brown.

Saddle

A black, saddle-shaped mark over the back.

Scenthound

Any of the breeds that hunt by smell, including Beagles, Basset Hounds, and Bloodhounds.

Semi-prick ears

Erect ears with only the tips falling forward.

Sighthound

Any of the breeds that hunt by sight, including Greyhounds, Whippets, and Afghan Hounds.

Smooth coat

A short, close coat.

Splayfoot

A flat foot with spread-out toes. Failing to keep nails short can cause a splayfoot and compromise foot health.

Sporting dogs

Any of the breeds designed to flush, point, and/or retrieve birds for hunters; also called gun dogs. Examples include Labrador Retrievers, Irish Setters, German Shorthaired Pointers; and Cocker Spaniels.

Standoff coat

A long, heavy coat that stands out from the body.

Stifle

The rear leg "knee" joint.

Stop

The angle between the skull and muzzle, more pronounced in some dogs than others.

Terriers

Any of the small to medium-sized breeds, mostly developed in the British Isles, designed to catch vermin.

Ticked

Small, isolated colored patches on a white background.

Topknot

A long tuft of hair on the top of the head.

Topline

The dorsal surface of the dog. In some breeds, the topline is level, and in others, it slopes up or down.

Toy dogs

Any of the breeds designed to serve as small companions to humans, such as Maltese, Yorkshire Terriers, Toy Poodles, Pekingese, and Shih Tzu.

Wheaten

A pale yellow color.

Whitelies

A white body with red or dark markings, as in the Pembroke Welsh Corgi.

Wirehair

A hard, crisp, wiry coat.

Wirehaired

A rough, wiry coat; also called broken-haired or broken-coated.

Working dogs

Any of the breeds designed to guard, pull heavy carts or sleds, or do other heavy-duty work, including Rottweilers, Doberman Pinschers, Siberian Huskies, and Great Danes.

Resources

BOOKS

All 87 Breed Dog Grooming for the Beginner.
New Jersey: TFH, 1995.

All-Breed Dog Grooming.
New Jersey: TFH, 1987.

Complete Dog Book, 19th revised edition.
American Kennel Club. New York: Macmillan, 1997.

Griffin, James M., M.D., and Lisa D. Carlson, DVM.
Dog Owner's Home Veterinary Handbook, 3rd edition.
New York: Howell Book House, 2000.

Kalstone, Shirlee.
*Poodle Clipping and Grooming: The International
Reference,* 3rd edition.
New York: Howell Book House, 2001.

Ogle, Madeline.
*From Problems to Profits: The Madson Management
System for Pet Grooming Businesses.* Revised Edition.
Madson Group, Inc: 1997.

Stone, Ben and Pearl.
The Stone Guide to Dog Grooming for All Breeds.
New York: Howell Book House, 1981.

Wilcox, Bonnie, DVM and Chris Walkowicz.
The Atlas of Dog Breeds of the World, revised 5th edition.
New Jersey: TFH, 1995.

WEBSITES

Find-a-Groomer.com
http://www.findagroomer.com/
This easy-to-use resource helps you locate professional
groomers in your area.

PetGroomer.com
http://www.petgroomer.com
This website has everything from lists of grooming
schools to specific directions on grooming different
breeds to advice on setting up your own business. An
excellent resource for groomers of any level.

The Groomer's Mall
http://www.groomersmall.com/index.htm
One-stop shopping for grooming supplies and more for
your pet.

Periodicals

Dog Fancy Magazine

Fancy Publications

www.dogfancy.com

Groomer to Groomer

Barkleigh Publications

http://www.barkleigh.com/groomertogroomer.html

717-691-3388

Groom and Board

H.H. Backer Associates, Inc.

312-663-4040

Organizations

National Dog Groomer's Association of America (NDGAA)

Over 2,500 members strong, the NDGAA has existed as a professional grooming association for over 34 years. They sponsor dog grooming seminars, trade shows, and grooming competitions and are committed to providing continuing education opportunities for their members. *Groomer's Voice* is the NDGAA's newsletter.

P.O. Box 101

Clark, PA 16113

724-962-2711

ndga@nationaldoggroomers.com .

www.nationaldoggroomers.com

Intergroom

This organization sponsors an international conference which features an extensive continuing education series as well as an annual grooming competition. Over 2,500 groomers attend the conference each year.

www.intergroom.com

or contact Christine DeFilippo for current conference information

76 Carol Drive

Dedham, MA 02026

781-326-3376

intergroom@msn.com.

Professional Mobile Groomers International, Inc.

Dedicated solely to mobile groomers, those groomers who make house calls in their own grooming vans.

www.petgroomer.com/pmgi.htm

or contact PMGI operations officer Pam DiRuggiero

1-866 BE MOBILE or 1-866-236-6245

MOBILEGROOMERS@CS.COM.

American Kennel Club

260 Madison Avenue

New York, New York 10016

or 5580 Centerview Drive

Raleigh, North Carolina 27606

919-233-3600

919-233-9767

www.akc.org

Index

Photo Credits

Paulette Braun: p. 37; p. 44; p. 110

All other photos by Isabelle Francais.

Cartoond by Michael Pifer.

Illustrations by Megan Krieg.